REMEMBRANCE

REMEMBRANCE

BY THE

REVEREND PROFESSOR EDGAR PRIMROSE DICKIE

M.C., D.D.

Chaplain to Her Majesty the Queen in Scotland

WITH A FOREWORD

BY

HIS EXCELLENCY BRIGADIER SIR BERNARD FERGUSSON

G.C.M.G., G.C.V.O., D.S.O., O.B.E.

Governor General and Commander in Chief of New Zealand

HODDER AND STOUGHTON

Printed in Great Britain for Hodder and Stoughton Limited, St. Paul's House, Warwick Lane, London, E.C.4, by The Faith Press, Ltd.

FOREWORD

I know from my own experience that it is not easy to find new things to say when we are invited to pay tribute to the dead of two major wars and of the many minor ones which have befallen us during this century. Repetition does not greatly matter; a liturgy does not grow stale with age: it becomes more hallowed every time it is said.

Yet somehow, in this moving collection of addresses, Professor Dickie has avoided repeating himself; and from the depth of his experience in the two great world wars, experience both soldierly and spiritual, he has found new reflections and new thoughts for us to mull over.

I was only seven and a half years old at the time of the first Armistice Day; and although I remember it dimly, I remember much more clearly the false report that flashed like lightning throughout Scotland four days prematurely that an Armistice had been signed. There were fewer telephones in those days, and of course no wireless; our rumour reached us from the railway station, so I fancy that the message ran down the old Glasgow & South-Western Railway by railway telegraph.

It is sobering to think how high a proportion of our present population will be totally unable to remember VE Day and VJ Day. It is therefore all the more important that the present younger generation, the generation which might have grown up enslaved, should know how and why the maintenance of their freedom was achieved, and at what a cost. It is important that we too should never forget. Alas, it is scarcely true, though we intone it once a year, that "at the going down of the sun, and in the morning, we will remember them". Those of us who suffered the closest bereavements probably do, but the bulk of us do not, or certainly not every day, as those words imply. Perhaps it would be morbid if we did.

The end of both those wars found the nation in a state of resolve: resolve that such a thing should never be allowed to happen again; resolve to see that it should not have happened in vain; resolve that every one of us who had been granted the privilege of survival – and God alone knows how the choice was made – should do our best to see that the flower of freedom which had survived the frost at such a sacrifice should flourish and spread. The times when we should really "remember them" are the times when for whatever reason we are in danger of betraying the chance which has now been preserved for us twice – twice at least. The reason is likely to be one of three: selfishness, sloth or cowardice.

And the other times when we should remember are on the formal anniversaries, such as Armistice Sunday, Battle of Britain Sunday, and here in New Zealand whence I write, as in Australia, ANZAC Day. Each Regiment also, each ship, each squadron, will have its special day: the anniversaries of Tobruk, Alamein, St. Valery, Gheluvelt, Festubert, Loos, Cambrai, Jutland, the River Plate, the Malta convoys.

My father used to tell of how, during the final weeks of the advance into Germany in 1918, he encountered a war cemetery made by the Germans, in which lay the bodies of Germans, British and French. At the head of the cemetery stood a cross; superimposed on the cross was a sword; and on the plinth was the inscription in the three languages: *The Sword Divides; The Cross Unites*. This is another thought which may sometimes help us in our decisions.

I for one will treasure Professor Dickie's book, with its

theme of *Haud Immemor* and its bidding of *Ne Obliviscaris;*
and in this I know I will not be alone.

BERNARD FERGUSSON

Government House,
  Wellington,
    New Zealand

CONTENTS

"A BOOK OF REMEMBRANCE WAS WRITTEN" — ONE

COLLEGIATE CHURCH OF ST. SALVATOR, ST. ANDREWS

REMEMBRANCE DAY; 8TH NOVEMBER, 1959

"Then they that feared the Lord spake often one to another : and the Lord hearkened and heard it, and a book of remembrance was written before Him for them that feared the Lord, and that thought upon His name. And they shall be Mine, saith the Lord of Hosts, in that day when I make up My jewels"
—Malachi 3.16–17

When the invasion of Europe began in June, 1944, Mr. Wallace, a coastguard, coming off duty that summer evening, heard the sound of innumerable aircraft passing high overhead. He called his wife and said simply, "This is it. . . . A lot of men are going to die tonight. We should pray for them." They knelt together to remember them at the throne of God.

Every year *we* remember, here in our ancient Church, the cherished centre of our corporate life. On panels round the Communion Table are inscribed the names of members of the University who fell in the First World War, and in the shrine by the pulpit are commemorated those who died in the last war; their names are written in a Book of Remembrance whose pages are turned week by week by the student-reader, so that the Roll of the Fallen is continually called.

Speaking on this occasion last year on "Attitudes to War", I was well aware that we ought, from time to time, to reconsider "Attitudes to Remembrance". Let us do that now.

1. There is always *the cynical attitude*. Writing of 1914 one author says "The causes of the conflict were demonstrably trivial and implausible". The ordinary people of Europe "could scarcely hope to benefit through victory in riches, security, culture, pleasure, advancement, or in any other way". As if the men and women whom we remember today were

striving for unimportant things like riches, pleasure, social advancement! The passage in the prophet Malachi from which the text comes offers a remarkable parallel. He is dealing with the complaint of those who thought that religion did not pay; people who had faithfully observed their "religious duties", even to wearing the sackcloth and ashes of humiliation and penance. Yet it is the arrogant and lax members of the community that do well. The cynic sees no worldly advantage in doing what is right; Malachi points to the final triumph of divine righteousness. When they say "It is vain to serve God" and ask "What profit is it that we have kept His ordinance?" he answers, "*No* profit to those who serve in that spirit; but as for those who fear the Lord and serve honestly 'they shall be Mine' saith the Lord of hosts 'in that day when I make up My special treasure' ". Even this cynical writer of today cannot help saying, "Many deeds were performed, all monotonously and astoundingly heroic". Indeed, if we go a little deeper, though still on the self-regarding level, and ask what to reply to those who say "Nothing is gained by war", we have to recognise that you and I are studying here, in liberty and quietness, because others fought for us. We live by the grace of the dead.

2. There is always *the indifferent attitude*. In the biography of Lord Goddard there is a moving description of the return of prisoners-of-war from captivity. At the port, a crowd of bereaved relatives surged towards the barrier, each one clasping the photograph of some boy whose fate was still unknown, and implored news. The other side of war is given by the experience of one of our own graduates. He carried with him from captivity a suitcase with the few precious belongings accumulated in five years; among them his box of surgical instruments, used for his fellow-prisoners and for his own wounds. At Liverpool docks he set down the case to greet his

relatives. When he turned to take it again, it was gone. There were people who had come deliberately to steal from returning prisoners-of-war. Sacrifice is sometimes forgotten – worse than that, it is exploited.

3. *The proud attitude.* It has been said that the note of grieving is passing steadily from these Remembrance Services to be replaced by a new sense of pride and thankfulness, and one writer (Alastair MacLean in *Radiant Certainty,* p. 70) illustrates this point by an incident that took place high up among the Border hills. A wandering scholar had been over-taken by the November night, and knocked at the door of a lonely cottage. A woman's voice called him to enter. He went in. She was seated alone by a little table which was covered by a white linen cloth. In the centre rested a cushion of blue silk. On it lay a few gleaming medals and beside them an open Bible. He suddenly remembered that it was Armistice Day. "I'm sorry", he said humbly, "I have intruded on your sorrow." But she turned to him with a smile. "No", she said, "that wound has been healed long ago and I am wiser now; for now I see my two boys as spirits immortal, radiant, safe with the Father and happy." Then, speaking more to herself than to the stranger, she added, "I too am a spirit. I must be worthy of my sons."

4. We have come to the fourth, *the Christian attitude,* that which most concerns us here. In it there are four special elements – gratitude, sorrow, sympathy, dedication.

i. *Gratitude.* When we give thanks in a Christian way, it is in the name of Jesus. Ultimately, it is for His sake that men took up arms to defend righteousness; His Cross is inscribed on our banners. The Heidelberg Confession shows true insight when it comes to deal with human goodness, sacrifice, kind-ness; for it sees them all as gratitude to God the Giver. The heading of this section on Good Works is simple: "Part

16

Three : Concerning Thankfulness". We remember that God is not the Giver only, but also the Redeemer. Our attitude to *His* sacrifice is quite different. It is unique; for we are not His comrades but his enemies. While we were *sinners,* Christ died for us.

ii. *Sorrow.* The cemeteries tended by the War Graves Commission on battle-fronts throughout the world; the memorials in churches and chapels and village-squares; the great public monuments and the shrines like that of Runnymede, commemorating those who have no known grave – these symbolise and express a nation's sorrow.

Today's remembrance should have the widest scope and reach. It should include Germans who were victims in German concentration camps as well as our own who died in them. In the summer this year I had the opportunity of re-visiting some of the leaders of the French Resistance, and there was brought to my notice again the pitiful record of young boys who gave their lives. Take one instance. Roger Rouxel was put to death at the age of nineteen. Here is his last letter :

My Dear Parents and Dear Little Brother,

I am writing you a last letter to tell you that I have been condemned to death. I am to be executed this afternoon at three o'clock, along with one or two comrades.

Please be brave, as I try to be. Forgive me for concealing from you the secret on which I was engaged, but it was impossible to let you know for I was sure you would have stopped me doing it.

I shall die thinking of you three, and at the last moment I shall have your names on my lips and your picture before my eyes.

Please keep my memory fresh at home.

iii. *Sympathy.* We should always have in mind that there

B

are many whose wounds are still fresh. Just as our students in enemy hands used to write that the hardest time of all to endure was the Christmas season; it spoke with almost unbearable eloquence of home; so there are many today for whom this season is the most trying of all the year. Here, therefore, our indifference must be combated. 'Is it nothing to you, all ye that pass by? Behold and see if there be any sorrow like unto my sorrow, which is done unto me." (Lamentations 1.12.) These verses from the book of Lamentations were spoken originally as a dirge over the fall of Jerusalem, the holy city of God, and its national sanctuary; and the exile of the people in Babylon. They may have influenced the "Second Isaiah", the prophet of the exile, in those very chapters which have been interpreted as a prophecy of the Incarnation and redemptive death of the Son of God. With reference to these verses from Lamentations Professor G. W. Anderson writes, "The agonised bewilderment which runs through all the poems has not destroyed God's purpose for His people".

iv. *Dedication.* This is the final purpose of remembrance. It should be the real outcome. It has been said of two men, father and son, that they had much in common, but one thing above all and that which mattered most. Roger Keyes, the planner of the raid on Zeebrugge, was known to be inspired with what was called "a desperate dedication". His son Geoffrey, best known for his attack on Rommel's headquarters in North Africa and his gallant end there, inherited that quality. It was dedicated ambition. Rightly, it was singled out by a posthumous award of the Victoria Cross.

The day of remembrance is a day on which we commemorate a *deliverance.* On the first Armistice Day, 11th November, 1918, Scottish soldiers, trained in the metrical psalms, turned naturally to them as giving the relief of utterance; and in many battalions besides my own that morning were heard the strains of the 124th Psalm. It was so also in this University on the 8th May, 1945. Students and staff assembled spontaneously in this place, as Bishop Kennedy's bell, "Katharine", rang out to announce peace in Europe, and we joined in the same psalm :

> Now Israel may say, and that truly,
> If that the Lord had not our cause maintained ;
> If that the Lord had not our right sustained,
> When cruel men against us furiously
> Rose up in wrath to make of us their prey ;
> Then certainly they had devoured us all.

This conjunction of deliverance and dedication is exactly in line with the teaching of the Bible. God is a God of action. He is in control of history : He orders the nations : *He* makes them and *He* breaks them. We notice how the first eleven chapters of Genesis are occupied with truths embodied in a tale concerning God and man ; but with the opening of the twelfth chapter we enter upon history. God speaks to Abraham ; He tells him not to search for truth, goodness and beauty, but to *act ;* to set out on a journey. So the writer to the Hebrews sums it up, "By faith Abraham obeyed when he was called to go out". So, later, the story of the deliverance from Egypt is followed by the dedication of the people under Moses. That deliverance occupies the place in the Old Testament which is to be taken in Christian hearts by the Crucifixion and Resurrection of Jesus. On the one side are the promises, the divine deeds, the call ; on our side is required obedience, dedication. Here lies the purpose of this day of commemoration. If dedication fails, all fails. "The righteous shall be had in everlasting remembrance. The memory of the just is blessed."

For their sakes, and in memory of them, we sanctify ourselves.

"A BOOK OF REMEMBRANCE WAS WRITTEN" — TWO

UNIVERSITY OF ST. ANDREWS; 10TH NOVEMBER, 1957

"And a book of remembrance was written . . . And they shall be mine, saith the Lord of hosts, in that day when I make up my jewels"—Malachi 3.16–17

Our Book of Remembrance lies here in the shrine behind the pulpit of John Knox. Over it is a window of remembrance. And in the tower of this church are the two bells, named "Katharine" and "Elizabeth". We have recalled how they were refounded at a time of crisis, in tribute to the members of the University who had volunteered for service with His Majesty's Forces, "forsaking all that was dear to them to fight for the preservation of liberty, truth, and honour". That was in 1940.

How much has changed since then! Indeed, one fundamental change began in the First World War. It is quietly recorded in a small, technical volume put out by the Stationery Office, with the title, *Science and War*. When a meeting was held to discuss a vital aspect of strategy, for the first time Lord Rutherford was late. He made his apology and added, "If I have really done what I think I have done this morning, it may be more important even than winning the war". He had taken one of the essential steps towards the harnessing of atomic power – and, though he did not see it as that, one of the first steps towards possession of the secret of mass-annihilation. We know that now. We know its implications. And yet man cannot abdicate. We have to agree with the President of Harvard when he says, "To be sure, there is the bomb, there is Russia, there are many other things such as there always are, to give the small-hearted pause; but despite the increased scale of such dangers, they are not new.

The possibilities to make a life, and to make a world, remain."

We recognise, of course, that the ways divide here; and good Christian people may take different roads. Some think that it is no longer possible to contemplate followers of Jesus Christ taking any part in war; that the preponderance of evil methods over the good ends to be achieved rules out the thought of participation; because when we enter on war, we enter on *total* war. It is right that this view should be stated, even on such a day as this, and right that it should be squarely faced. For is this not true? Look solely at *one* set of facts and you become pacifist – the wreckage, the loss of life, the moral deterioration of participants, the incalculable destructiveness and horror of the instruments at our disposal. Then look solely at *another* set of facts and you doubt whether pacifism can ever be the last word – the loss of freedom, suppression of the truth, the fettering of religion, the corrupting of children, the cruelty of dictators, the concentration camp. Many who were members of this University and other universities owe their lives to the dropping of the bomb on Hiroshima, because they were in Japanese hands at the time and their death had been decreed and planned. Had it not been for that special deliverance, their days were numbered, as were, beyond a doubt, the days of hundreds of thousands of American soldiers and sailors and airmen committed otherwise to the over-running of the Japanese forces by repeated and costly assaults. It is impossible to draw up a calculus, in terms of numbers saved by the swift surrender, and numbers destroyed by the bombing. The tragic feature still remains – the innocent multitudes sacrificed. Let us remember them also on this day of Remembrance.

It is perfectly true that the Christian pacifist weakens his case when he pretends to believe that Nazi Germany and Imperial Japan (and other nations like them) are no worse

23

than the Western democracies; and the Christian militant spoils *his* argument when he takes as his guiding principle the Norfolk toast: "Our country! In her intercourse with foreign nations, may she always be in the right; but our country, right or wrong!" Here is a tension from which there seems to be, as yet, no escape; for the convinced pacifist must recognise now that, if he choose passive resistance and martyrdom, the consequences are not confined to his own life. Nor will his children necessarily share his martyrdom with him, as often was the case in the early Christian Church. Instead, in the modern villainy, they are kept to be indoctrinated with hatred of the very faith for which he died. If this tension cannot as yet be resolved, it is of the highest importance that Christian people should not unchurch one another because of the views which they sincerely hold. Both witnesses are needed in the Christian Church.

It is fortunate, then, that all can unite in Remembrance. It is always good to remember sincerity, and courage, and sacrifice. The commemoration covers two World Wars. It is hard for this generation to realise that during a large part of the First World War our campaigns were fought entirely by volunteers. In the panels behind our Communion Table we have the names of men who left these halls of study because of the nation's need and the threat of world-wide tyranny: who for us and for our freedom, and for the deliverance of the earth, gave their lives. Indeed, since Time marches on relentlessly, there may be many here who are unaware of the large number of students who, though entitled to claim exemption from service in order to complete their courses, nevertheless chose voluntarily to leave these halls and take up arms. One of the symbols by which we commemorate those who, as the French say, "remained at the Front", is the silence in which we joined this morning.

24

The other symbol – the scarlet poppy – comes also from that long conflict in France and Belgium from 1914 onwards. In Flanders especially the red poppies grew so thick that one could watch the machine-gun fire cutting them down in little narrow swathes. Inevitably, these flowers of sleep became the symbol of Remembrance of the dead; those blood-red flowers the symbol of sacrifice. Those whom we commemorate were almost all very young men and women, and we might think of that hymn of sacrificial love which ran, when it was first written:

> When I survey the wondrous Cross
> Where the *Young* Prince of glory died
> My richest gain I count but loss
> And pour contempt on all my pride.

It was altered – rightly, I think – to read simply:

> On which the Prince of Glory died

because the sacrifice of Jesus is for us all, sinners of all ages; but the original version is a reminder that we chiefly mourn the sacrifice of youth, of *young* men and *young* women.

In that second war there was not the reckless squandering of lives which marked its predecessor. In general, war-memorials indicate this. It is evident on our Town War Memorial, where, in a little while, we join the citizens of St. Andrews in an act of remembrance.

You may be aware that the difference runs the other way in our University. Between the wars the numbers on the matriculation roll had increased. But there is another reason for our second Roll of Honour being larger than our first. A number of young men passed through the Air Ministry short course; spending six months here as full members in our

25

corporate life – strenuous days, but wonderfully happy, memorable days. Alas! so few survived!

Our own personal gratitude as members of a University which played a not ignoble part in the struggle for liberty is in the Book of Remembrance which lies here in its shrine. It was unveiled by Queen Elizabeth, now the Queen Mother; and its pages are turned, one every Sunday, by the student-reader, so that the Roll of the Fallen is continuously called. It contains one hundred and sixty-five names. As we now join in our hymn of Remembrance I recall for you the words which are written on the first page:

The righteous shall be in everlasting remembrance.
Praise ye the Lord!

How bright these glorious spirits shine!
Whence all their white array?
How came they to the blissful seats
Of everlasting day?

Lo! these are they from sufferings great
Who came to realms of light,
And in the blood of Christ have washed
Those robes which shine so bright.

REMEMBERING IN CHURCH — CHRISTIAN REMEMBRANCE

UNIVERSITY OF ST. ANDREWS; REMEMBRANCE DAY,
11TH NOVEMBER, 1962

Once again we have kept the silence as it was observed in its beginnings – at the eleventh hour of the eleventh day of the eleventh month. It symbolises the silence that fell on that first Armistice Day in France and Flanders. On that long unbroken front from Switzerland to the North Sea, where the guns had thundered well-nigh continuously for four years, the noise suddenly began to die away, and by the appointed hour there was an uncanny hush, so unaccustomed that it seemed almost eerie and frightening. Then there came a ripple of cautious cheers, that swelled into a clamour of rejoicing.

The silence was reminiscent of earlier silences, like that fateful moment when the barrage lifted from the enemy front-line and there was a space of soundlessness : and as the men prepared to climb out of the trenches to advance, they might hear a lonely skylark singing in the blue above them. John Masefield wrote of that moment imperishably in his book *The Old Front Line*. "The men of the first wave climbed up the parapets, in tumult, darkness and the presence of death, and having done with all pleasant things, advanced across the No Man's Land to begin the Battle of the Somme."

In the earlier post-war years, when the Armistice silence was observed, not on Sunday but on the actual day, the eleventh, the result was most impressive. In town and country, movement ceased. The people in the city street stopped and stood still ; the plough-boy came to a halt in the furrow.

Something was lost, perhaps, when the pattern was changed so that the silence was observed on the nearest Sunday morning. But something was gained. It is better in Church.

28

The *Christian* character is emphasized and perpetuated.

For us also the silence recalls the general silence of church-bells during the Second War. From the time of the Battle of Dunkirk they were kept to give warning of imminent invasion. With the others, our own bells in this tower above kept silence and were first rung (by Mr. Snow) on V.E. Day, the day of victory in Europe. The "Katharine" bell had been found to be faulty and had been silent for two and a half centuries. It is pleasant to recall that the imperfection was remedied in war time. It was a symbol of confidence, like that of Jeremiah, while a political prisoner during the siege of Jerusalem by the Babylonians, buying a piece of family property and declaring confidently that the Chaldeans will one day be expelled and his land liberated. The Court minute of St. Andrews University, dated 10th June, 1940, speaks of undertaking the re-founding of the bells in 1940, a time of crisis. The minute ends with the words, "The cost of the restoration has been borne by Mr. James Prain as a token of gratitude for selfless endeavour and noble example".

It has often been observed that war brings out the worst in the bad people and the best in the good. It certainly reveals the coarseness in brutish men. There were those who wrote brutishly of war, denigrating the fighting men and attributing none but selfish motives to people and nations. I think of them as of the railway employee whose job it was to tap the wheels of coaches to see that they rang true. One day he reported that a whole line of coaches must be taken off; there were flaws in all the wheels. The superintendent soon guessed the explanation. It was not the wheels that were faulty, but the man's own hammer. The cynic, it has been said, is a man who judges the character of others by his own. We can forget that type, and remember the opposite, those whose natural goodness flowered under stress.

In the first years of the two minutes' silence, equally impressive to many was the return to activity. Pedestrians in the street and vehicles on the road resumed their course: the plough-boy continued his furrow. Thus, over against the silence, we have to place speech. Ours is a period in which we have to learn to use language aright. For example, a radio critic, speaking of the cruelties inflicted on Jews in German concentration camps, ended by saying, "Here we have a vivid picture of the horrors of war". These were not the horrors of *war*; the evils of the concentration camps were perpetrated, not by us but by others: and they made it inevitable for many Christian people that they should engage in war to end them and to prevent their recurrence. We must be very careful to use language aright. "Would you be prepared", pacifist friends often ask, "to press the button that might involve the death of a hundred thousand people?" That question can be understood aright only if we ask the other question, "Would you be prepared to press the button to *deliver* fifty million people from death and horror?" The pacifist solution would be an easy way out if it were a choice between *two* things; and it is quite frequently claimed that this is, in fact, the position; that we have simply the old tragic feud between Castle and Church: the antagonism between Fear and Faith. The metaphor is inadequate. We have a *triad*: Castle, Church and concentration camp. Besides Fear and Faith we have to reckon with Love – love that dares everything to deliver our pitiful fellow men from the slave-camps, or to save the succeeding generation from having to endure such servitude. Whatever answer is given, the Christian must make very sure that he is asking the right question.

I have said that by remembering here in Church we emphasise and preserve the *Christian* character of the act. There is a special interest for us in the legend of a vision that came to the Pictish king. It was a story told by the monks in St. Andrews, with reminiscences of the Damascus Road and of the Emperor Constantine, of a vision of St. Andrew challenging him and saying, "Angus, Angus give ear to me, the Apostle of Christ, Andrew by name, sent to defend thee. Behold the sign of the cross of Christ in the sky; let it go before thee against thine enemies." The king saw the white cross against the backcloth of the blue sky; and so that saltire became the standard of Scotland.

How is our commemoration properly linked with the Cross of Christ? It must be linked somehow, or it will become a mere form of hero-worship – the praise of famous men. The link appears to me to be this : What we have in the life of Jesus as recorded in the Gospels is the record of One who was *in* history and yet not *of* history; One who lived an earthly life that embodied and exhibited all the ideals of human nature. What we call "the Christian life" was shown to be a genuine possibility. Since then Christ was *in* history, but since we know also that He was not *of* history, He is worshipped; He is not pattern only, but Saviour. When people say, "He is just like one of us", the sufficient answer is to enquire, "Like which one?" Yet we need the encouragement of recalling that, being in history, He is also pattern. Man must endeavour to lead "a Christ-like life".

I select three points in which this is seen :

1. *Dedication.* In itself, this is a victory over evil. We see it in men like our own Doctor of Laws, Lord Wavell, of whom his biographer has said, "No blow, fair or foul, military or political, ever got past the shield of his integrity". This is the kind of person whom we remember in the silence.

2. *Courage.* The "lovely virtue" of Barrie's Rectorial address – and we recall that specially just now. It is precisely fifty years today since the bodies of Captain Scott and his

companions were recovered from the ice of the Antarctic. Courage is not always displayed in such dramatic circumstances as those of Scott's polar expedition. It is told, for instance, of one humbler participant, on the very fringe of war, a member of a concert-party going to the Middle East, that he lay asleep in his bunk, hour after hour, waiting for the explosion that would kill him. I think that he was one of the bravest of men, for when it came to his turn in the ship's concert, he did his act even when he was terrified. He was afraid, and that is something that he could not control : but he played his part, and that was something that he *could* control. That is the real courage – even when afraid, still to be able to make the body do what you order it to do.

3. *Sacrifice*. The word comes easily to our lips when we are thinking of the Christian who died in war. But what of the reprobate? what of the "natural man"? – and there are plenty of *them* in battle. They are not automatically sanctified. That would be a Moslem supposition, not a Christian view. Even of a last-minute repentance, the truth has perhaps been best stated by Augustine. Commenting on the story of the penitent thief on his cross, he says, "There is one instance in the Bible of last-minute repentance, that none of us may despair ; but only one, that none may presume".

Nevertheless we may believe that when there was true dedication, there was true encounter with God ; perhaps, too, whenever there was courage ; certainly where there was selflessness and sacrifice. Much depended on the attitude taken up by the person concerned. There is a vast distinction between the infliction of a death and the laying down of a life. And that distinction has an important bearing on our acts of Remembrance.

We like to think that the redemptive power which was supremely present in the self-sacrificing love of Jesus is present in *all* self-sacrificing love. We speak of "that love which He enkindles still, in hearts that Him adore". But there is an antithesis as well as an approximation. Since the love of Christ for the world is the love of a Saviour for sinful men, it is different, not in *degree* but in *kind* and, therefore, because it is divine love, it is love in which men and women can trust to the very uttermost. Whatever happens to this troubled world, *that* love will never fail. It cannot fail. It gives that security and peace which even the highest of human relationships can never yield. "Not as the world giveth", Jesus said, "give I unto you. Let not your heart be troubled, neither let it be afraid."

c

REMEMBERING AT EASTER

BROADCAST ADDRESS IN CHILDREN'S HOUR TO ALL REGIONS;
25TH MARCH, 1951
FROM CATHCART CHURCH, AYR
Leader of Worship: The Reverend Alexander Hutchison
Conductor of Music: James R. Liddell
Organist: Hunter F. Thomson
Under the auspices of Ayr and District Sunday School Union
President: The Reverend R. D. M. Johnston, M.A.
The Lesson, from St. Luke's Gospel, chapter 24, verses 1–6a,
13–16, 28–31, was read by Frances Banks, one of the children

Let me tell you of a strange adventure which came to some gallant people. Their city was in the hands of a brutal enemy. They made up their minds to set it free, and to set it free from within.

We have heard of "Underground Movements". This was really one : they couldn't use the streets to keep in touch with one another, because enemies would notice them, so they went underground and used the waste-pipes that ran under the city streets for miles and miles. Some of the pipes were wide, but some were very narrow indeed, and might be choked with mud. To go one mile, a patrol might take ten hours, fifteen hours, even twenty hours.

One day a patrol succeeded in crossing the whole city, underground, and had only to clamber up the last drain and out of the manhole in order to deliver the food and the ammunition which they had brought with them. Alas! Unknown to them below, an alarm had sounded in the streets : the manhole was closed by its thick, heavy stone cover. They beat against it in vain. No sound could get through to their friends who, from time to time, would be waiting for a signal. Not even their radio was of any use : for the sets employed by their friends above in the city were small and of little power. Must they go wearily back again and report their failure and their misadventure?

We must leave them there for a minute or two. (But it's going to be a story with a happy ending.)

Do the flowers feel something of the same despair in winter, trapped beneath the hard, frozen earth?

Did the women of the Bible story feel like that as they made their way this Easter morning to the grave of Jesus? They asked one another, "Who will roll away the stone?"

Did the disciples feel like that on the road to Emmaus? (They walked, and were sad.)

In each case, something was going on unseen and far off. The men beneath the pavement hit on a fantastic plan. In despair they sent out a radio message to London, nine hundred miles away, where ears were listening day and night. The powerful set in London magnified the tiny sounds. They were understood. Word was quickly sent back to the people *above* ground, across those nine hundred miles. They heard. They raised the cover. "The stone was rolled away."

Today the sun, far off, is sending light and warmth that will soften the hard soil and call the flowers into the upper world again. (*That* message comes, not nine hundred miles, but one hundred thousand times nine hundred miles.)

The women did not know; but God had been working from the other side. The stone was rolled away. Jesus was alive again!

For the two disciples on the road, God was not even far off; not ninety million miles away. Jesus *"drew near,* and went with them". They didn't know it was Jesus; for they were full of their own troubles; but I'm glad that the disciples did the right thing. Though they didn't know who He was, they asked Him to stay and have supper with them. And, as He broke bread – then they knew. He had done this before, just like that. It was the Lord!

Like the men of the underground, like the women at the grave, we find at Easter time that the stone is rolled away. Two things are conquered for us.

First, sins are forgiven because Jesus died for us.

And death is beaten because Jesus rose for us. Death has no power any more.

> Trees will be a-living and a-waving,
> When I am dead;
> Birds will be a-living and a-singing
> When I am dead.

It is an old Negro spiritual; and then comes the joyous, unexpected ending; for the singer has remembered that Jesus is risen triumphant, and all is well.

> Who will be a-living when I am dead?
> *I* will! *I* will!

These two things are conquered. But more than this: Two things are gained. Like the flowers in the earth, we come out at Easter time into a new and marvellous world. Two things are ours for ever.

First, victory is secured, because Christ is victorious. You will have power, Jesus told His disciples, "power from on high". Wrong things will not be able to touch you if you have this power, nor do you harm any more.

Second, is peace, peace that the world cannot give, but only Jesus; peace that the world cannot take away.

> Christ is risen!
> He is risen indeed!
> ALLELUIA!

THE SCHOLAR AND THE SOLDIER

The Collegiate Church of St. Salvator, St. Andrews;
9th November, 1958

"These all died in faith not having received the promises"
—Hebrews 11.13

When news came to St. Andrews of the death in battle of one of her scholars, his former tutor wrote, in sorrow and vexation, "What had you to do with Mars the god of war? – you who were dedicated to the Muses, nay, to Christ Himself?" The scholar was Alexander Stewart, the young archbishop, the founder, with Prior Hepburn, of our St. Leonard's College. He died on the field of Flodden. His tutor was Erasmus, who could not understand what learning had to do with warfare.

Let us dwell for a little on this theme of *The Scholar and the Soldier*. Take a modern instance also. It comes from Sir John Kennedy's book *The Business of War*. When the evacuation from Dunkirk was completed his unit was stationed near Cambridge and the officers received notable hospitality from the colleges. It was very evident, however, that military talk was not welcome in the Senior Common Room. "The dons", he writes, "did not regard war as a serious business, or as an interesting subject of conversation."

No doubt there was a quick change in the attitude of the Cambridge dons. The seriousness of the situation was soon evident, even to the dreamiest occupant of an ivory tower. The cynicism that could regard as "uninteresting" the over-throw of France, the advancing tide of barbarism, the sacrifice of thousands to defend us, the heroism of the little ships – that cynicism was no doubt half pretence. Many of the same cynics were soon to be caught up in war and to give a satisfactory account of themselves! But – are we still in danger?

40

Are we perhaps *always* in danger? – the danger that we may take our comforts, take our privileges, take our peace for granted and forget the cost? A visitor was shocked at his experience in a cinema in this country. The film was the story of prisoners-of-war in Japanese hands. At the sight of men staggering after torture, a considerable section of the audience reacted with merriment, as if this were comedy, having no relation to actual happenings. Battle scenes provoked laughter. Why? Because, I suppose, of the conditioning of audiences to *spurious* comedy and *unreal* horror – audiences which yet may become awesomely hushed, even tearful, over the most superficial sentiment. A great mass of people have forgotten, or want to forget, war and suffering and sacrifice. There is urgent need to maintain our two minutes' silence and our Remembrance Day.

It is appropriate that we should remember the work of the University units who, with the representatives of all the students, have laid wreaths on the war-memorial for those who died in their own branch of the services. The Navy: the first casualty suffered by the University during the Second War was a graduate who went down with the *Royal Oak* in Scapa Flow – Hugh Stewart, Bachelor of Science, Instructor Lieutenant in the Royal Navy. The Air Force: a pathetic feature of our Roll of the Fallen is the high proportion of very young officers of the Royal Air Force. Many of them came to the University for a period of six months under a scheme devised by the Air Ministry. Of the earliest courses very few came through alive. The Army: since it is their jubilee year, we ought to think particularly of the Officers' Training Corps. War-time training was severe. All members (and membership was compulsory) were required to do two hundred and ten hours of training each year. No wonder that they received the accolade from a visiting General who

41

reported that the St. Andrews contingent was qualified to meet, if need be, fully-trained enemy troops and at least to give a good account of itself. The cadets were, no doubt, frequently greeted with the condescending smile of those who thought of them, and spoke of them, as "playing at soldiers". The attitude would have been very different had they foreseen how many of the men of whom they spoke so lightly were soon to give their lives on their behalf.

And we ought to remember those who suffered through being prisoners-of-war. Here again our involvement was very considerable. In 1940 when the 51st (Highland) Division was surrounded at St. Valery many members of the University were serving with it and passed into captivity for five weary years. The University at once launched a scheme whereby they might be enabled to continue their studies in a modified way, so relieving the tedium of their fate and turning it, so far as might be possible, to profit. The University Court gave an initial contribution of twenty-five pounds to buy books and they were never required to make another, for funds flowed in steadily from students and friends. St. Andrews led the way in this, to be followed (but never superseded) by the comprehensive scheme organised by Lord Lindsay of Birker. We remember those who died as prisoners-of-war or in the final forced march when the allied armies were closing in, and those whose health was undermined by the privations of long captivity.

This is a day on which men's minds turn naturally to reflection on the different attitudes towards war revealed in our own time. They have been sharply focused in David Howarth's book *The Sledge Patrol*. In Greenland, where these events took place, there was a unique situation, presented by the very conditions of life in the Arctic. In the experience of the Eskimo, to meet a hostile man was just as unlikely as to meet a friendly bear. Men were *friends*: that was the condition of survival. Into this situation came the German patrol. When they killed Knudsen, he was the first man in all the recorded history of the North Greenland coast who had died at the hands of a fellowman. The tragedy of Cain was re-enacted. Over against that we set the next significant event. At one point two Germans returned to base because they had been "unable to shoot" – a curious explanation which perhaps had never before been brought to a German officer. *Something of the Arctic had got into them.* In this long fight, this warfare in miniature, in North East Greenland, diverse opinions were revealed concerning the morality of war. There was Schmidt, the Nazi leader, whose dream of German greatness had been proof against the arctic charm. There was Ritter, the naval officer with the German party, whom Arctic beauty, which he had experienced once before in Spitzbergen in time of peace, led back to the paths of God. There were Poulsen and his companions, opposed to the German party; they *loved the arctic peace and made war to preserve it.* And there were the Eskimos, whose whole world was pitched in the Arctic splendour and whose morality was in the Sermon on the Mount.

This is a day, however, not of controversy on the ethics of war, but of Remembrance: and with the recollection of the dead we are bound in loyalty and gratitude to remember also the maimed and the crippled of both wars. The British Legion still cares for many of them, from both periods; so do the regimental associations. In this district we feel a particular responsibility towards the local regiment, the Black Watch or Royal Highlanders. These men not only proved themselves good soldiers: they have also had their shrewd observers. One of them is on record from the First World War. Encouraging a raw recruit in the front-line trenches he says, "It's far waur

43

for the Germans. . . . You, as a British soldier, are fechtin' conscripts, pressed men, but the Germans will be fechtin' men wha are fechtin' o' their ain free will." "Like the Black Watch", he added, "the finest soldiers in the world." It seems incredible to many today that we fought so large a part of the First World War with volunteers only. Yet, I believe, had there been no conscription in 1939, men would have volunteered just as they did in 1914 – but in 1939 they had no say in the matter. There was indeed little to choose between the citizen armies of the two wars.

The soldier-scholar has a special part to play. And he has played it well. Of others too it might be asked, "What have you to do with Mars, the god of war?" What of the farmer at the plough asked to give his barn for storing arms before D-Day? He said he would plough to the end of the furrow and give his answer when he passed back again. The answer was "Yes". D-Day came, but by that time both the farmer and his wife had been executed. In our natural eagerness for ease and comfort and a quiet mind, we dare not push out of sight the realities of war and suffering and sacrifice. There is urgent need to maintain our two minutes of silence and our Day of Remembrance.

REMEMBRANCE AND DEDICATION

COLLEGIATE CHURCH OF ST. SALVATOR, ST. ANDREWS;
10TH NOVEMBER, 1963

45

"I thank my God upon every remembrance of you"
—Philippians 1.3

Remembrance Day. It began as Armistice Day. At the eleventh hour of the eleventh day of the eleventh month in 1918, the fighting ended on the Western Front. That moment made, of course, an indelible impression on all of us who were student soldiers of the time, "seconded" from our studies for four years with the services.

What were the attitudes of men and women on that far off day?

First and foremost was that of *relief*. The danger was over: the threat of further suffering was gone. Many were poised to attack early next morning. For us, therefore, it may have meant that we went on living instead of dying.

At home there was widespread *rejoicing*. How right that was! – even when it was exuberant.

For others, there was a renewed surge of *sorrow,* for the day brought home to the bereaved that for *their* loved one there was no return. For them, rejoicing was muted and subdued.

It is this third response which is specially in our minds today. Indeed it is surprising that Remembrance Day has been perpetuated. Even the Second World War is history now; and the first is in the dim past. But again how right it is that we should hold our ceremonies of recollection, of gratitude, of dedication. Here we lay our wreaths beside the memorials of our forefathers, and after this service we join with the people of the town in a wider recognition of courage and sacrifice.

What should be the notes sounded at such services?

Thanksgiving, certainly; perhaps thanksgiving first. When the greatly loved Principal David Cairns was dying, he said to his son, "Let it be thanksgiving! Not too much about the grass withering and the flower fading. Everybody knows about that. I had a lot to be thankful for. So let it be praise!" So with us, let it be praise.

And first, praise for deliverance. It is true that many of our likeable Christian pacifists tell me that this is a false note. They advocate submission, rather than deliverance by the use of force, and they tend to sum it all up in contemporary terms by crying "Better red than dead!" We sympathise with them and honour them for their feelings, often courageously expressed; but it seems a foolish slogan. The hope is, presumably, to save the next generation, or a later one, to live on as Christians when the Communist domination has collapsed. They envisage a kind of return of the people of Israel from Babylon. It would not be so. We know what the Communist practice is. It contemplates indoctrination of the young, till children hate their parents, and loathe all that Christianity stands for. We are right to give thanks for past deliverance from all tyrannies; for on the other side we remember words of Edmund Burke, "All that is necessary for the triumph of evil is that good men do nothing".

Praise, next, for courage – often the courage of simple men and women, never tested in this fashion before. One half of the First World War was waged by this country with volunteers alone. The cynics are confounded. There was little brash jingoism. As a recent writer has said: Though it was taboo in the ranks to confess it, these volunteers were there because they wanted to protect the people of their particular glen, hillside, parish, village, township; they were defending their homes. (*The Scotsman Weekend Magazine,* 21st September,

1963.) And in the later war? It is inspiring to read the modest account of Australian nursing sisters in Malaya. Three simple words strike home. Someone had to stay behind to look after the wounded. It meant imprisonment in Japanese hands. None could tell for how long : none knew the conditions except that, for women, they would be unspeakable. The writer says, simply, unemotionally, "We all volunteered". (Miss Simons in *While History Passed*.) When we speak of courage we must, I think, realise that very few, only the unusual kind of person, came through their ordeals without moments, at least, of acute apprehension; but courage is often just that state in which the will can make the body obey against all instincts. Lord Ismay tells how he took Winston Churchill to one of our airfields during the Battle of Britain. "It was impossible", he writes in his *Memoirs,* "to look at these young men, who might within a matter of minutes be fighting and dying to save us, without mingled emotions – of wonder, gratitude, and humility". Every year we commemorate that battle. We remember the sacrifice. Do we always remember the challenge to be worthy of it? There is a sequel to Lord Ismay's story of that night. "As the evening closed in, the fighting died down, and we left by car for Chequers. Churchill's first words were : 'Don't speak to me; I have never been so moved'. After about five minutes he leaned forward and said, 'Never in the field of human conflict has so much been owed by so many to so few'." These words, spoken in private so soon after a moving experience, were spoken again in public and have become part of our heritage.

After thanksgiving, *Penitence*. That ought to find a place in our remembrance. We all share in guilt. Every nation has done many things, and failed to do many other things, and so brought war nearer; and all share the guilt of those evil things to which men are driven simply to survive in war. The same

48

agony of decision affects the individual soldier and the responsible statesman. Yet we must be realistic, or our penitence may become a parade. When a letter to the national press affirmed that Germans and Japanese are much the same kind of people as we are, it drew the realistic reply: Some of them, yes; but "did we set up Belsen and Buchenwald and Auschwitz and Ravensbrück? Did we bayonet our war prisoners to death?" The truth lies elsewhere. All of us are in desperate need of God's grace because all are sinners; but men's sins are not all the same; and it is our own that we ought to confess. These, it may well be, are drunkenness, immorality, irresponsible living, failure to lead when we were given the opportunity, as never before, by the sacrifice of those whom we remember at this time.

After penitence, *the Conquest of Hate*. Hatred did not last long, if it ever existed, in the minds of the fighting men. In the First World War we had the characteristic comment of one of them: "I feel sort of sorry for those Germans", and in the second this admirable scene: One moonlit night in the Square of Cologne, one of the downcast inhabitants, probably surfeited with British Army rations thrust upon him by his conquerors, still weighted down by his country's defeat, was encouraged by a Scottish soldier saying, "Och, dinna tak it to hairt, man. Your lads fought grand." For all men this conquest of hate is a Christian duty.

An American play presents the theme of an old woman in the Far West meeting the son of a man who had long ago killed her husband. With a sudden fierce hatred rising in her heart, she seizes a shot gun to kill the lad; but just at the moment when she is going to fire she seems to hear something. She drops the weapon and tells the boy to be gone. "What was it you heard?" he asks; and she tells him that it was the voice of her own son, who died in the war; and what the voice said was, "While you go on hating, my wounds will never heal".

49

Fourthly – and this must be the climax and the purpose of it all – *Dedication*. Have we proved worthy of the sacrifice? We know of the dedication of men and women in the services. Field Marshal Lord Alexander once said, speaking of the American Army, "They are splendid comrades, splendid"; and he added reflectively, "You see, at times a soldier's duty is to obey and die. We all have to remember that."

There are, indeed, cynics still, as the war books show. They were there already on the first Armistice Day. A member of a noble house records that, on hearing of the cease-fire, his unit "all felt flat and dispirited. We decided that a party and some gambling might cheer us up." Scottish regiments, I am proud to say, gathered under their commanding officers and, with an engaging and memorable naturalness, sang together Scotland's Psalm of Deliverance:

Now Israel may say, and that truly,
If that the Lord had not our cause maintained;
If that the Lord had not our right sustained,
When cruel men against us furiously
Rose up in wrath to make of us their prey;
Then certainly they had devoured us all . . .

Therefore our help is in the Lord's great name,
Who Heaven and earth by His great power did frame.

From the innumerable instances of dedication, take only these two: One writer saw an ambulance draw in. There was a gaping hole in the cabin. The driver tried to open the door, and suddenly fainted. "I opened it", the writer goes on, "and he fell into my arms. His left foot was gone." A shell had landed near the car: he had driven the last mile with his other foot on the accelerator. Three badly wounded men were saved.

The other instance from the Royal Navy. During the evacuation of Crete heavy naval casualties were sustained in preventing a sea-borne invasion of the island. (They knew all about the danger. As one of the destroyers steamed out of the harbour at Alexandria, an able-bodied seaman was blowing up his life-belt. "This", he said, "is all the air-support I'm likely to get on this trip.") Army spokesmen said that the Navy could not be called upon to suffer any more losses. Admiral Cunningham would not listen. In memorable words he said, "It takes three years to build a ship, but three hundred years to build a tradition. The Navy will go."

"Good Generals", it has been said by one of them, recalling the one thousand casualties each day at Alamein, and the sixty thousand on the first day of the Somme, "good Generals are reluctant to sacrifice our troops on a gamble, partly because we have so few to fight with, partly because we lack ruthlessness in this matter. If we are to lose valuable lives we must be sure that the sacrifice is worth while." This, then, is part of our dedication. We shall endeavour to ensure that the sacrifice has been worth while.

When the British Army was evacuated from Dunkirk, it looked, as someone said, like a defeated rabble. And Adolf Hitler said scornfully, "We shall not hear much more of the British in this war". He was wrong. Is it to be said of us now in peace? Or have we the courage and the determination and the soul to defy the contempt of others, and to prove them wrong once more?

Do we feel that our part is small, lacking influence and example? Remember then the words of one of the honorary graduates of St. Andrews University, Henry Sloane Coffin, speaking at Yale. He quoted: "The pillars of the State are shaken. What can a good man do?" Then, leaning over the pulpit, he said quietly, "He can go on being good".

"I thank my God upon every remembrance."

GOD IN HISTORY

BRITISH LEGION SERVICE. CAIRD HALL, DUNDEE
REMEMBRANCE DAY; 9TH NOVEMBER, 1947

53

There are gathered here both old fighters and young fighters – and perhaps a sprinkling of those who managed to be both, adding a little to their age in 1914 lest the war should be over by Christmas (they need not have worried) and knocking a few years off in 1940, and getting away with it both times. Many of you must have taken part in the final assault for the for the liberation of Europe and will realise how the enemy made one supreme mistake. He turned Europe into a vast fortress, but it suffered from one weakness. It had four strong walls but it had no roof. It could be attacked from above. It was four times as foolish, really, as the Maginot Line.

That is a parable. It will not do to leave out the heavens. It was a *religious* war that you fought. Nothing less. Everything of value was at stake. Of course we were fighting for our existence but I counsel you never to listen to those who will tell you, as they tried to tell us, that you were tricked into fighting for national or political ends alone. In all that happened it is impossible to miss the hand of God.

In the Spring and early Summer of 1940 He permitted us to be carried to the very rim of the dark abyss. Our prayers became very earnest, very real, in the days following Dunkirk. Our fighting men were never more courageous – on the high seas, in the burning sands of the desert, in the skies over the city of London. Our people in their homes and in the war factories were more deeply devoted to their tasks than ever they had been before. And from the very rim of the abyss God, in His grace, plucked us back.

Three thoughts, I believe, are uppermost in our minds today.

54

First, *a solemn sense of the Divine presence in history.* We have watched, in awe and wonder and solemnity, the working-out of God's terrible judgment. We saw, in the space of a very short period as history runs, the coming of a grim retribution. The enemy air-force was the instrument that was to dominate the whole world by terror from the skies. And from the skies came the destruction, terrible and pitiless, which annihilated the power of the enemy to make war.

"They that take the sword shall perish by the sword." We know a little of the dread lengths to which lack of religion will carry a nation, even the nation of Martin Luther, a nation that once had been in the forefront of religion. We have learned something of those hidden transactions in the secret cells of concentration camps; and have shuddered as we passed that building in Brussels, in Paris, in Breendonck, where unutterable things were done to men and women and children. Death or torture was the fate of those who, in Germany itself, protested against such things in the name of Christ. In the hour of darkness they found their consolation where they had always sought for it – in their Bible and their God.

The second thought must be one of *Thanksgiving.* For Scottish people it will always be expressed most clearly and most movingly in the words of the Psalm of Deliverance, sacred to our fathers of the Covenant on the hills and in the hunted glens; sung by Scottish soldiers all along the front line when they gathered at eleven o'clock in the morning of the 11th November, 1918, to hear the news of the Armistice and the end of their bitter strife; sung also in many gatherings of Scotsmen by sea and on land at the end of this last war.

> Ev'n as a bird out of the fowler's snare
> Escapes away, so is our soul set free;
> Broke are their nets, and thus escaped we.

55

Therefore our help is in the Lord's great name,
Who heav'n and earth by His great power did frame.

With proud thanksgiving we remember the courage of many
people, not alone in the fighting services. We think, for
instance, of those in the occupied countries who might be
faced suddenly with an ultimate choice. An Allied airman,
perhaps, or an escaping prisoner-of-war, appealed to them for
shelter. In a few seconds they had to make the decision; and
how often they decided courageously, though, as they well
knew, the forfeit was their life. Above all we remember those
who are not to return to us : their young lives were the price
of the liberty which we have won. We thank God upon every
remembrance of them. We think now in deep and affectionate
understanding of those who recall them in their homes.

For their sakes, it would not do to halt there. There is a
third thought in our hearts today – that of *Dedication*. As a
nation we have done much in our history that we should not
have done; very much. Even in the midst of that fiercest
struggle for our existence, we were often guilty of self-seeking
and pettiness and pride. There were times, indeed, when we
sought God very earnestly; but we have a very long way to
travel before we can claim to be a Christian land. Even that
lovely thing, the fellowship of battle, is in danger. It seemed
once to be the one sure gain from war; and now those who
have returned from the services are afraid that this may be
too easily lost. "We are not on the same side any longer", they
say. "We were all on the same side then; but now it's everyone for himself." How tragic if that should be the outcome
of peace! The man who wrote one of the earliest accounts of
Arnhem tells how in that life which was nearer to an animal
existence than anything he could have conceived, the more
savage the fighting became, the more civilised the men seemed

to become. Stripped of everything that appears essential for decent life, men began to show such gentleness and friendship as would have made them almost uncomfortable back on the station. (*Arnhem Lift,* page 95.)

Or I think of the young Frenchmen of the Resistance. You remember them – no uniforms, precious few rifles. Their terms of service had been very simple – no fixed rates of pay, no pension, and torture if they were caught. And they volunteered in tens of thousands.

Surely we shall not lose such courage and such dedication because peace has come; because we have emerged victorious. Peace is a dangerous season. Remember always that the younger people are watching you – watching with admiration, though they may not show it outwardly – and you can lead them as you choose, well or ill. Will you lead them into the ways of Jesus Christ? Pray earnestly that we do not betray them. Tried and tested under God's hand in the darkest hours and now brought out into the light once again, will you offer yourselves afresh in His service? You have it in your power to build up a safe and lovely land.

BATTLE OF BRITAIN SERVICE

St. Giles' Cathedral, Edinburgh; 17th September, 1961

The First Lesson was from 2 Samuel 23.13–17, and was read by the Flag Officer, Scotland, Vice Admiral Sir Royston Wright, K.C.B., D.S.C., R.N.

The Second Lesson was from Revelation 7.9–17, and was read by Air Commodore The Duke of Hamilton,

K.T., P.C., G.C.V.O., A.F.C., D.L.

The Officiating Ministers were

The Reverend C. Y. McGlashan, Q.H.C., D.D., Principal Chaplain Presbyterian, Royal Air Force

and

The Reverend W. M. Laing, D.D. Moderator of the Presbytery of Edinburgh

"Other men laboured and ye are entered into their labours"
John 4.38

In the spring of 1940 at Dunkirk, the last little boat had taken
on the last shipment of weary soldiers. Then the Commander-
in-Chief took with him the senior naval officer and recon-
noitred the long stretch of coastline for the possibility of a
few more survivors. As a last precaution, General Alexander
raised his voice and cried, "Is anyone there?" He was
answered by the challenge of a German sentry. The long
night of darkness had closed down on Europe. Now the fate
of our own country lay in the hands of the Royal Air Force.
The Battle of Britain was about to begin.

The Battle of Britain is still on. To survive, we must be
more than courageous: we must be dedicated.

People often say, unthinkingly, "War settles nothing". True,
it produces its own crop of tragic and seemingly insoluble
problems; but at least it may settle whether we should be free
men or slaves. At least it delivered us from that night of darkness which settled on Europe then. Of the battle which took
place on the field of Poitiers in A.D. 732 and broke the Moslem
power, Edward Gibbon wrote: "But for it the interpretation
of the Koran would now be taught in the schools of Oxford
and her pupils might demonstrate to a circumcised people the
sanctity and truth of the revelation of Mahomet". The sacrifices of our own day decided for us that we should not be
degraded to the level of *Mein Kampf* or the system and prac-
tices of Bushido. This is a day of remembrance and thankful
acknowledgement.

Other men laboured and we are entered into their labours. Others died: we live. It is a law in human history that we reap harvests which others have sown. There is a solidarity in all progress. The Christian Church lives today by the labour and patience and sacrifice of the past.

Take two pictures, one in Scotland, the other in Africa. We think of St. Ninian in his little church of white stone in Galloway, a pioneer and alone. There was not even a Scotland. In the land north of the Solway there was no kind of unity, only a multitude of tribes. Even the Roman legions did not penetrate far. The Cross often goes far beyond the sword. The Christian missionary went where the pagan army had never ventured. It was so also in Africa. Miss Mary Slessor of Calabar penetrated into dark places where the British troops hesitated to go. In many parts of the African interior even today the only troops you will encounter are the Troops of Boy Scouts established by Christian missionaries!

One more picture from the past. As children we used sometimes to hear the minister say in his closing prayer, "Take us to our homes in safety". Perhaps we wondered why he used these words. For us it was an easy and happy scamper home after the Benediction! The way home was indeed far too unadventurous, almost *dismally* safe. But the petition came down to the minister from the days of the Scottish Covenanters when our forefathers had to go by stealth before dawn; to gather in some lonely cleft of the hills; and to post sentries with muskets while they worshipped, not knowing whether, after worship, they would ever see their homes again.

People like these laboured in their time, dedicated to liberty and to freedom of worship, and we are entered into their labours. We reap where others have sown. This afternoon we are thinking of that which comes home very intimately to our own business and bosoms. We are recalling the sacrifice of men without whose gallantry we should not be here. We live

61

by the grace of the dead. Our enemies once said – and perhaps we too lightly believed them – that our youth was decadent. Sociologists used to ask despairingly what future could be expected for children born in the stress of the war years of 1914 to 1918 and the troubled period which followed. What became of these children? We know the answer. In the Battle of Britain it was such children who guarded our skies and shielded our land and saved the world for civilisation. Though highly skilled by then; disciplined physically and mentally; and (though all light-heartedly) completely dedicated to their historic summons, they still seem, to us who look back, very young. There is an epitaph, in another sphere of similar gallantry (the Marine Commandos at Vis) which brings out this tragic quality of our remembrance:

> Here dead we lie because we did not choose
> To live and shame the land from which we sprung.
> Life, to be sure, is nothing much to lose;
> But young men think it is, and we were young.

People often ask in perplexity why Heaven allowed so many to be withdrawn prematurely from the joy of life. We know part of the answer when we remember that this world is a place for the fashioning and testing of character; a vale of soul-making. God does not need the time that we need to test a character. Only He can know whether service here or service yonder is better for a man. Indeed, we may ask, what bigger thing could God have used them for? A padre tells of a father who came with the news of his son's death in action. The father's face was white and set, but his head was carried proudly and there was a light shining in his eyes; and all he said was, "I had great dreams and ambitions for my boy. I was perhaps too proud of him. But I had never dreamed of anything so big as this." Can we not say, with John Bunyan,

"Now just as the Gates were opened to let in the men, I looked in after them; and behold the City shone like the sun. . . . And after that they shut up the Gates: which when I had seen, I wished myself among them."

There were other heroes of the Battle of Britain, some discovered and honoured; others – many more of these – nameless, unknown and unsung; doctors and nurses; fire-services; the alert Observer Corps; the gallant and steady members of the Civil Defence, some of them girls, others elderly and even aged men and women, never trained for war, nor ever with a thought of engaging in it, till it was forced upon them. But their hearts were right, and therefore all went well with them. There is little doubt that every natural feeling of apprehension and anxiety and mental anguish went through the minds of every one of them, but all these were put down by firm resolve : with a light heart they went to their dangerous work; conspicuous for courage where courage became a commonplace. Heroism has a timeless quality : it is part of the eternal world. It is right that we should remember, and it is right that we should dedicate ourselves again, here in the presence of Almighty God.

We read together the touching story of the well at Bethlehem. That moving incident occurred in the middle of a grim campaign. David was a refugee; had gathered his tiny band for safety in a cave; was pressed on every side by an overwhelming company of the enemy determined on his capture and his death. It happened that his hiding-place was close to his own village of Bethlehem and his thoughts turned back, as men's thoughts will on the eve of battle, to his home and his boyhood; and he longed to drink of the clear, cold water of the well round which the boys used to play. But Bethlehem was in the hands of the enemy. Then we read how these gallant men – so few! against all the might and panoply of the Philistines – these few break through and bring back some of the precious water, won at the hazard of their lives. To David now this water is a sacred thing, too precious for his use. He offers it to God. I regard the story of the Battle of Britain as the "Bethlehem story" of our war – the impossible task, and the men, the chosen few, who achieved it by the sheer power of faith and courage. Their victory should be received by us in the spirit in which David received the sacrifice of those men who brought the water from the well of Bethlehem : a memory so precious must not be profaned. It is a thing too great for men : it must be consecrated to God.

If we remember those lives which have most clearly found the meaning of existence, which have penetrated to the Wisdom of God, we shall find in every case that their secret lies in sacrifice. We look at fathers and mothers who have given up all their chances of having an easy time in order to make things easier for their children. Or we think, as we do specially today, of those who understood life so well because they were called so early to hazard it in war. Their life was completely satisfying because it was woven throughout in sacrifice. And now, so long as we live, there is no breath of freedom that we shall ever draw, no bread that we shall ever eat, that is not purchased by the lives of those men. Strangest of all is this, that we learn the final secret of life from One who gave up His life at the age of three-and-thirty. "I am come", Jesus said, "that they might have life, and that they might have it more abundantly." He came that we might have – not happiness necessarily, nor wealth, nor success, but – life, the endless thing which runs out beyond every perplexity and every sorrow, because it comes from God and goes back to God.

Other men laboured, and we are entered into their labours. The righteous shall be had in everlasting remembrance. Praise ye the Lord !

REMEMBRANCE AND RESURRECTION

University of St. Andrews ; 7th November, 1948

"I know that my redeemer liveth"—Job 19.25

Job was facing the last enemy; and we cannot pretend, even
with our Christian faith, that death comes into our midst as
anything other than an enemy. It stands in front of all, as one
of the facts of this present world, with the weaknesses and
pains which lead up to it, or the sudden blow which brings
it about. The pilgrimage of this life leads us up to a gateway
where the door opens only to those who are going out, and
allows no others to see what lies on the far side.

Today it is not of a far off story that we are thinking, nor
of the sacrifice of strangers whose names are *only* names to us,
but of brothers, friends, sons. We live by the grace of the dead.
Blood was sprinkled on the lintel and on the side-posts of *our*
houses, throughout all the land; and because of that the Lord
passed over *us*. We go in safety.

In his darkness, Job sees one guiding light. "I know that
my redeemer liveth." That word has a strange history. It
seems curious that the precious name "redeemer" should once
have meant "the avenger"; the man whose duty it was to take
revenge in blood for the killing of one of his family. Yet
perhaps not so startling after all. That other precious word,
the "Cross", was once a word of shame and infamy. The very
mention of it made men shudder.

In the first stage of the word "redeemer" it meant the
avenger in a family feud, the leader of a vendetta. By the time
of Job, however, it had passed into the second stage, and,
with the Second Isaiah, who used it of the Lord, it was a
favourite name even for the Holy One of Israel who would

redeem His people from captivity. For Job it means already a vindicator, a champion in the face of a common enemy. The idea of the family is not, I think, altogether lost; for death comes as the oppressor of the human race, the enemy in whose presence we are all united; an enemy who seems to bring an end to noble dreams and brave companionships.

In the final stage of the word's history it is used of Jesus. This is He of Whom Job dimly dreamed. There are many bold, defiant, daring utterances in the Old Testament about the final victory of goodness; but the Old Testament would be a sad book if we were to come to the last chapter of Malachi and, turning over the page, find that this is all; the rest blank. This vindicator, dimly dreamed of by the best of the Old Testament writers, we have seen, and He is Jesus.

There are two chief ways in which Jesus vindicated our trust in God. Again and again, in every age, there is thrown out a twofold challenge. God allows so much sorrow and suffering, men say, that either He is not a loving God, *or* He is not an all-powerful God. Either He does not want to make us happy, or He cannot. Let us see how Jesus justifies the ways of God to men.

1. Jesus vindicates *the love of God*. There are certain facts which seem perpetually to challenge this love. Of these we are very conscious this morning. War is such an outrage on human personality. It seems inconclusive : it may be followed by economic ruin for victors and for vanquished. It leaves its legacy in the ruin of veracity, and the cheapening of human life. It means a lost generation of leaders. On this no one needs to dwell in this place, where sacred memorials remind us of past sacrifices. But we cannot build up a theory of life on isolated facts. If we wish to know about God we must look on *all* the evidence. There are sad facts, unutterably sad; but there are happy facts also; and sometimes – often – these are

unutterably happy. How sweet life can be! How sweet are its companionships! And we owe them all to the same love which we are challenging. The untimely breaking of the bond of love is a perplexing thing, but it was God who made that love possible. The Lord hath taken away – yes; but it was the same Lord who gave, and gave so generously, so marvellously. Blessed be the name of the Lord! We know that we shall "one day stand together in a brighter dawn".

Even when we have given thanks for the incredible wonder of human affection, we have made only a beginning. There is still the fact which is the measure and the pledge of God's love, the fact of Jesus. It is to Him that men turn when they meet the cruel aspects of life. Here is one who has passed through the dark rooms; a man of sorrows and acquainted with grief. He knew God best, and He said that God is one whom you can trust through everything. "Father", He said, at the darkest moment, using the word of love and perfect understanding, "Father, into Thy hands".

Once, when His own disciples were terribly perplexed, Jesus said to them, "What I do you know not now, but you shall know hereafter". Though we never know anything more than this alone, we know enough. We know that our redeemer liveth. And He is Jesus. We may live our lives out without fear. One day we shall look back and understand. Meanwhile we can wait for the explanation, knowing that if Christ is in it all is well. Christ lives and reigns.

2. We turn to the other question. Jesus answers also the challenge thrown out by the dark experiences of the world against *the power of God*. War is a costly way of settling disputes. Yet there are costlier ways. There is something which is to be hated more than war – unrighteousness. There are things greater even than peace – and truth, justice and kindness are among them. "War settles nothing" we hear people

68

say; but a settlement made by unrighteousness is worse than no settlement. Nevertheless, even when oppression has been defeated, there remains that from which many suffer today, a sense of frustration, the fear that the future may yet be decided by injustice, because injustice is far seeing and calculating and crafty. Those who are in the right rely too easily on their rectitude and go about unarmed. Their very strength is their weakness. A man in the wrong knows that he must look to his weapons; his very weakness is his strength. The good man is never prepared for combat: the other is always ready. Are we justified, then, in believing in an ultimate decency of things? God loves His children: is He able to deliver them? Again, the fact which is decisive is the fact of Jesus. And we ask in which direction this points. At the moment of the crucifixion it looked as if it pointed towards the darkness. His enemies, when they had brought Him to Calvary, cried out that this was His final defeat; a sign that *they* had been right all the time. Death on a cross proved that. Even His friends whispered that this was weakness, failure, disaster, the end. Today, Jesus, because of His Cross and Resurrection, is the power of God unto salvation. Through the remainder of the New Testament, and through all Christian experience since, there rings the triumphant peal, "He is able! He is able!" He is able to keep us from falling. He has measured His power, you notice, against a far more fearful thing than death. For death is not the terrible thing that once we imagined it to be. It is not the end, but the glorious beginning for the children of God. But that other thing, the evil that is in mankind, could that be the dreadful end of all, leaving a soul in eternal darkness? Jesus has pitted the power of God against this. He has completely changed our ideas of the meaning of power. Suppose that we picture God's greatness and majesty to a sinful soul; that we tell how God has

69

made this world and all that is in it, and that all may pass away at His command: He can create and He can destroy: that His hand can crush all that rises against Him. This picture of God may drive the sinful soul to despair. But we can give, instead, the picture of the power of God as we see it in Jesus. This power has made new men and women; it has changed their souls. And that is the hardest task in all the universe. To create a new world is nothing in comparison with this – the remaking of a soul. There is no limit to the power of God.

As we think of those whose names are engraved on our memorials and deeply graven in our memories, our hearts are filled with sorrow and with longing. The beloved places know them no more, but those places which they once loved do not forget them. Every dear corner of the land is a Book of Remembrance:

> Twilight and Tweed and Eildon Hill,
> Fair and thrice fair you be:
> You tell me that the voice is still,
> That should have welcomed me.

Where shall we look for reassurance, when darkness threatens the world and when longing tugs at the heart? We look to that victorious proclamation of the New Testament – "He is able". There is nothing which the power of God cannot do; no task which we may not commit to that power with perfect confidence. He is able to keep them to the uttermost – in danger, in sorrow, in all the fears of the unknown – able to keep them to the uttermost that come unto God by Him.

DEDICATION SERVICE: THE RED CROSS SOCIETY

SOCIETY

St. Giles' Cathedral, Edinburgh; 14th May, 1961

When people gather together in services of remembrance and dedication, inevitably their thoughts go out, if they have passed through the rigours of war, to the gracious splendour of the work done by the Red Cross. Time and again, the wounded owed their lives to your ministrations; the prisoners-of-war owed their sanity to your faithfulness in caring for them; the refugees found life and purpose and new hope because of your devotion to them in their pitiable state.

Some years ago, while making a study of vagrancy in Scotland, I came across one of those maps drawn by the brotherhood of tramps, and passed from hand to hand, intended mainly to act as a guide to the most promising houses for alms, and to warn against those at which a hostile reception might be anticipated. It had the usual "conventional signs" to indicate these places. One of the signs with unwitting humour had the memorable connotation "Religious but kind". There is a whole sermon in that one word "but".

Religion that does not issue in kindness is not religion. The Epistle of St. James has been declared as of doubtful value, and been called an "epistle of straw" because it appears to teach that we can save our own souls by good deeds; but it may be that the author assumed as common knowledge among his correspondents, and took for granted, the kind of Christian theology expounded by St. Paul, and then went on to show how important it was that there must be no mis-understanding about this. Faith is vital; of course it is; but faith without works is not faith at all; not vital but the very opposite; faith without works is *dead*.

"Please", asked the little girl in her prayers, "please make

all the bad people good, and all the good people *nice*." She
meant "kind", "gentle", "considerate", "pitying".

My theme is "Faith and Pity". The two go together.

Can you have kindness without religion? – the pity without the faith? We all know the "decent pagan"; know him
and even respect him. Luther called him the *bonus vir*. The
bombing of London brought him to notice in thousands.
People who made no claim to be Christian put many to shame
by their courage, their kindness, their gentleness. When you
praised them they would say they were just doing the decent
thing – though by a significant illogicality sometimes they
would say they were only doing the *Christian* thing. We
should not ignore nor despise this "natural goodness". One of
the most outstanding theologians in Europe, Dr. Karl Barth,
makes an odd contribution to this question. After examining
the parable of the Good Samaritan, he concludes that there
are three elements involved in the help that we give to our
neighbour: 1. We help him in order to offer him the word of
God; 2. We help him in order to signify to him *God's* help;
3. We help him in order to authenticate what we have to say.
I confess to some difficulty here. I even incline to whisper,
"What surprising things we theologians can say!" For it does
not seem to me that the Good Samaritan did any of these –
offer the word of God; seek to signify God's help; try to
authenticate what he had to say. He just buckled to and
helped where he saw that help was urgently demanded. Anything else would have been artificial; pious humbug, more
in keeping with the character of the priest or the Levite.
Barth's reading of the parable seems to carry us very far away
from the simplicity of the Gospel. Like you, in your universal
mission of kindness, the Good Samaritan was moved simply
by the plain need of a helpless human being in trouble.

Suppose, however, that pity were all. Thinkers like Fichte

and Hartmann have made profound attempts to establish morality without religion. It would not do. (Mrs. Knight, of Aberdeen, in our own time and less profoundly, has tried to argue for "goodness without God". Would I venture to call the attempt a kind of Mrs. Margaret Knightmare?) No; pity alone is inadequate. Indeed, it can easily produce a sense of inferiority in the one who is assisted and too often a sense of pride in the one who condescends. Pity must be accompanied by faith – not faith that is obtruded, but faith that glows and burns within.

There are some things – the most valuable of all things – which this "natural pity" cannot supply.

1. It cannot give *continuance*. It has been said that men do not build hospitals because of charity, but in self-defence. If a man comes to your door with small-pox, you cannot let him in; you cannot kill him. So you provide a hospital; and you do this to protect yourself. That is the view of one man. He is, as you see, a cynic – and Sir James Barrie once described a cynic as a man who, mean himself, makes himself the measure of other people. The cynic's theory will not do. It breaks down when we consider the nurse. It cannot account for one who gives her life to care for those who have to be "turned from our doors". When the great plague descended on Alexandria, sweeping away thousands, the Christians, we read, visited the sick without fear, and died beside them rather than flee. "Quite the reverse was it with the heathen", writes one who was there. "They abandoned those who began to sicken, fled from their dearest friends, threw the sick, when half dead, into the streets, and let the dead lie unburied." The sympathy, courage and humanity displayed by the Christians made a profound impression on the non-Christian world. Pity alone will not give continuance. That calls for the faith which *you* have, faith in the value of

74

every human being; and that, in turn, comes from the Christian conviction, "A thing of price is a man, because for him Christ died".

2. Pity alone cannot give *power*. i. It cannot give power to perform what love enjoins. We either bear the burdens of others, or we add to them; for we cannot live to ourselves. No one goes to Heaven or Hell alone. He lifts his weaker brother with him or he drags him down. "We then that are strong ought to bear the infirmities of the weak, and not to please ourselves." ii. Nor can it give power to break the dominion of hatred. "Humanism" is not enough to challenge the terrors of our age. We have seen in Europe in our time Fascist and Nazi and Communist in control; we have witnessed calculated malignity on a world-wide scale. Only a power that comes from above can break these chains. We live in a materialistic age. Dr. Bronowski can actually say that the discoveries of this century have changed all the basic concepts of human life. That is not genuine scientific talk, but merely a scientist's mumbo-jumbo. *No* change has taken place in the most vital of all our concepts – the difference between right and wrong; between love and hatred; between God and man. And all these three are closely interlocked. Your service is an active proof and demonstration of that truth. You stand for the eternal difference between right and wrong; for the ultimate triumph of love over hate; for the claim of the Lordship of God on the obedience of man.

3. Pity alone cannot give *pardon*. Humanism, with all its sincerity and sympathy and charity, cannot speak the word that is needed by the soul. What if we fail in our earnest endeavours? And we all know, Christian and non-Christian alike, that if we are setting any kind of worthy standards, we are bound to fail and fall short. When that happens the good pagan has no other resources. When he fails, he fails for ever.

75

Non-theistic ethics cannot speak the word *pardon*. Justice, yes! and restitution of what has been unjustly gained, and a fresh attempt to do better, but not the divine forgiveness, only the certainty of failing again and again. The Christian knows that when he fails, as we shall all fail, again and again, he can plead the sacrifice of Christ for him.

> O Saviour, I have nought to plead
> In earth beneath or heaven above,
> But just my own exceeding need,
> And Thy exceeding love.

The cross on your world-famous emblem has no religious significance, because of your co-operation with many who are of a different faith (you are members of a great company of one hundred and twenty-seven million); but for us gathered here in this building, a Cross has a vital meaning, nevertheless. So often, faith has faltered and pity has wearied. Here again they are renewed. Here you have come to seek the blessing of God on all your work, that work which has given hope and, indeed, life to hundreds of thousands overwhelmed by catastrophe of nature, or in prison-camps; to victims of plague and war and cruelty. Here you take strength from one another engaged on the same holy work. Above all, you take strength from One who knew the sufferings of man's body, and the anguish of man's spirit; One who understands the weakness of our faith and the frailty of our pity; yet not only pardons these but singles out the little unremembered kindnesses and in the Day of our Judgment brings them to the notice of our Father as services offered in faith and pity to none other than Himself.

"Inasmuch as you have done it unto the least of these, you have done it unto Him."

BATTLE OF BRITAIN SERVICE

ROYAL AIR FORCE, KINLOSS : AT ST. LAURENCE CHURCH,
FORRES ; 16TH SEPTEMBER, 1962

A visitor to a Highland manse told me of an experience he had many years ago. It was Communion Sunday morning and, after breakfast, the household assembled for family worship. The white-haired, patriarchal minister was in the habit of reading straight through the Bible, a chapter each day, from the first verse of Genesis to the last of Revelation, without any omissions; and it so happened that the passage that day was a forbidding one, a genealogical table. Even his musical voice could hardly give meaning to the formidable list of *begats;* and the visitor was thinking that this was dry fodder for the spirit in preparation for the Lord's Table, when the old man called them to their knees in prayer. "We thank Thee, O Lord", he prayed, "that the names of all Thy children are written one by one in Thy Book of Life."

Our first solemn duty this morning is to recall with proud thanksgiving those who gave their lives in the Battle of Britain. Without their sacrifice we should not be here today as free men and women.

It is the special day of the Royal Air Force and we all rejoice that you who belong to this station have been made Freemen of Forres. For many of the congregation, no doubt, that battle is not so much a memory as a part of history. The younger ones have heard about it or read about it. Now even the spate of war books seems to be drying up. Some of them have been good, some bad, a few evil. Some of them have misrepresented the fighting-men, or regarded it all with cynicism, or were written simply to make money out of others' agony. J. M. Barrie once said that a cynic is "a man who measures the conduct of others by his own standards". The cynical attitude forgot the strain imposed on any peace-loving, gentle personality, when he had to dedicate himself, not only to dying – for many, that was *not* the hardest part – but even to *killing* in defence of those things that death cannot conquer nor time destroy.

That touches on one of the real agonies of the Christian who is summoned to wage war. In that shadier type of war book the theme of *futility* recurs again and again – as if nothing had been accomplished by years of strife. One writer cannot visualise any cause worth dying for. (He really means, of course, worth *his* precious life.) So for him death is sheer disaster. Freedom from slavery or from the threat of the concentration camp for his loved ones – these do not appear to have occurred to him as worth dying for. That is characteristic of the cynic. *Of course* there were mixed motives and *of course* all Italians were not Fascists, all Germans were not Nazis, all Japanese were not sadists; but the Fascists, the Nazis, the sadists were in control, and dismissal of concentration camps as propaganda, and the horrors of the infamous railroad as exaggeration will not do. The evidence, unhappily, is there in photographs, in the memories of those who liberated those places of infamy, in the broken and shattered bodies of those who came out of them, and in the dreams of many who suffered in the inhuman toil of that railroad.

The *good* war books should be read – especially by those for whom the war is only history. We forget too soon; even those who lived through it forget too soon both the heroism, and the barbarity which that heroism opposed. I spoke of the barbarity. There is no need to dwell on the heroism; but it is right to remember that those involved were largely *young* men and women, of the average age, perhaps, of this congregation. Responsibility was thrust on them prematurely. The commander of a motor torpedo boat has been described in these

79

illuminating words: "A young man of great age". These young men smiled at the attempts to make heroes of them. There is one typical picture of the tail-gunner, on his long flights over Germany, punctuated by sharp spasms of terror, reading the magazines which told about their "nerves of steel", in order to assure himself that he wasn't scared. Or the infantryman, knowing before an attack that, in a few hours now, one in ten will have looked his last upon the sun. And there were times, as in an opposed beach-landing, when for a little while the average expectation of life was calculated at three minutes.

Sometimes I think that the best of all war books is the Old Testament. It is strange indeed that there should be so much about fighting in a book about God. Yet a man might steel himself, before going into action, with verses remembered from his Sunday School teaching – "The Lord of hosts is with us: the God of Jacob is our refuge", or "Quit you like men, be strong". And mothers with their children in the air-raid shelters would find comfort in saying: "I will both lay me down in peace and sleep, for Thou, Lord, only makest me dwell in safety". It might almost seem that there are parallels here for every crisis. At Dunkirk we thought of the crossing of the Red Sea: in the Battle of Britain of the little-known verses from *Ecclesiastes* (9.14–15). Above all, perhaps, we re-read the story of the well at Bethlehem, 2 *Samuel* (23.13–17). That story has remembrance at the heart of it, and dedication.

Old Testament Remembrance Days recalled the crossing of the Red Sea as their special day of deliverance – as we look back to Dunkirk, to the Battle of Britain, to El Alamein: to the Third Battle of Gaza or the victory of the Marne. The Jewish Church has a tradition from which we may learn. It conceives God as saying, of the crossing of the Red Sea,

"Can you *rejoice* when so many of My own children perish?" Pharaoh's brutal soldiers were *His* children! So our remembrance covers all, even those who were most guilty. That does not mean that we fail to distinguish. There are just causes: and there are causes that are most unjust. There is aggression and there is resistance to aggression. But as Christians living in the era of the New Testament and under the grace of the divine redemption, we are called both to remembrance and to forgiveness.

We think of those fighter-pilots of the Battle of Britain, flying alone against frightening odds, as a symbol of the fate of man himself amid the emptiness and mystery of the universe around him. Over against that awesome picture of human loneliness, the Christian sets the assurance that God is with us, because God was in Christ reconciling the world unto Himself. It is *His* world, and His sons are safe in His keeping. There is much that is mysterious. "Now we see not yet all things put under Him", says the writer to the Hebrews; but he quickly adds "But we see Jesus". That is sufficient for hope to arise again victoriously. Ours is an age of anxiety, even, some say, "an age of terror". Then let us recall that serene inscription in the porch of an English village church, set down when the country was ravaged by its worst civil war.

In the year 1642, when most things sacred were either demolished or profaned, this church was built by one whose singular praise it is to have done the best things in the worst times and to have hoped them in the most calamitous.

"Wherefore, seeing we also are compassed about with so great a cloud of witnesses . . . let us run with patience the race that is set before us, Looking unto Jesus."

81

F

"GREATER LOVE HATH NO MAN"

University of St. Andrews; Remembrance Day, 12th November, 1961

One special memory comes of age in this year. It is twenty-one years since the evacuation of Dunkirk, the epic of the little ships and the weary men.

The calmest of all was the blinded soldier who took a sailor's hand and followed him with silent trust into the deep water.

At the same time, while they waited patiently for rescue, a chaplain gathered the shattered remnant of his unit and offered prayer. Suddenly, hundreds of others, who saw and understood, could be seen kneeling in the sand-dunes, an unending vista of bared heads, as they bent in silent worship.

So one special *memory* comes of age.

At that time one special *text* came alive. It is one which is engraved on many war-memorials: "Greater love hath no man than this, that a man lay down his life for his friends".

First, it is a reminder of the sacrifice which a man will sometimes make eagerly for a brother man – a Sydney Carton in literature, a Captain Oates in very fact.

Then, because we are thinking of a Christian memorial, we recall that the words were spoken by Jesus Himself. We think of a sacrifice which was made for more than a circle of friends. He died for mankind. "Ye are my friends", the passage continues, "if ye do whatsoever I command you." Gradually the Christian Church realised that they were witnessing to something far more wonderful than even the heroic sacrifice of man for a brother man: they were testifying to the love of *God* – in Christ, who died for all the world.

There are perplexities here, too, as well as assurance; for there must be many names on many war memorials of those who knew little of the "Saving Name" of Christ. We cannot believe, nevertheless, that in the moment of their death they were beyond the scope and efficacy of His redeeming love. Where there was courage and integrity "We may not so belittle Christ", says Dr. Micklem, writing on *The Doctrine of our Redemption,* "as to question His power to save". "The grace of God is too large for our finite minds."

On this day some of us are remembering the end of the First World War when, at eleven o'clock in the morning on the eleventh day of the eleventh month, abruptly the guns ceased fire and there was an uncanny silence, then a ripple of cheering that ran along the front line trenches as we realised that the war was over. Many more are thinking of May, 1945; but for most of you here this morning even that is history!

Let me tell you a little more of what happened in this ancient chapel, built in 1450, witness of much history, when victory in Europe was proclaimed. Shortly before eleven o'clock that morning of the 8th May ("V.E. Day"), students and staff gathered in front of the church, where the thanks-giving of the University was to find its first expression in the worship of God. Ranged along the three sides of the quad-rangle, they waited in silence until the hour had struck upon the bell "Elizabeth of St. Leonard's". A few minutes longer they waited; for our other bell, "Katharine," had a special part to play. It is the bell of Bishop Kennedy himself, the founder of the College of St. Salvator. He had it cast in 1460. For two and a half centuries it had been silent (except for a trial stroke at the conclusion of the South African War). But since 1940 and till 1943 *all* church bells had been silent except for the peal to celebrate the victory at El Alamein in 1942. They were kept ready to give warning: they were to be the signal that invasion was imminent. Both our bells were refounded in 1940, at a time of grave crisis; and the Minutes of the University Court of 10th June say of "Katharine" that the bell "is restored in the hope that it may next sound to celebrate a righteous peace and to welcome the students who return to the University after serving their country in the present struggle against oppression". On that morning, in the hushed quadrangle, the first careful strokes were like the tolling of a passing-bell; it was our *In Memoriam;* then the bell eased on its bearings and swung into its natural rhythm and there sounded over the old College Tower the peal of victory and thanksgiving.

"Greater love hath no man than this, that a man lay down his life for his friends." The Christian valuation of human life – this is by no means a simple matter. There can be no hesitation in the minds of good men concerning the wanton contamination of the atmosphere or concerning the concentration camps ("those suburbs of Hell", as Pierre-Henri Simon has called them); but there are the perplexities for ever being raised by the apparent fact that the military condition entails its own sins; that vice foments war, virtue does the fighting. Our war-time dilemma was expressed in this way: There is no one too young to be expendable. That's what this war is. And there is no one so old or so maimed that they should not be cherished. That's what it is about. A few individuals disagreed with the first part. They believed that their own gifts were too precious to be expendable – their hands as musicians, their inspiration as poets – and they took refuge in neutral countries. We have there the age-old problem of Art and Goodness, said to be solved by the people of the Basque country who gave up Art because life was too short to practise both Art and Goodness. The thought of "expendable" youth is most relevant in a University community. In our own in St. Andrews a large proportion of the names on our

Roll of the Fallen belong to young men who came to the University for a six months course before training as fighter-pilots, bombers and navigators. It could be said that the nation's decision was to call upon all its youth in defence of the old, the maimed, and all who were threatened by the prisons and the gas-chambers of totalitarian dictators.

There were other realms of courage and sacrifice than the fighting services. In the incredible, cool bravery of the Fire Service and in Civil Defence the same approach was manifest. "It was queer", says one, "and strangely comforting, that in the midst of all that destruction, we set so much value on a single life and that a dozen might be risked to save it, and yet we set so little value on life that we would risk twelve valuable, healthy, skilled lives for one old woman of ninety, or one paralysed child".

It was very noticeable to those who served with the British Expeditionary Force in 1940 how the attitude of Lord Gort, a great commander and a great Christian, went through a significant and appropriate change. So long as victory was possible he never spared his army; but as soon as he realised that victory was not possible in that campaign – and it has been said that he realised this earlier than the War Councils in London and Paris – he determined to save his army.

The contribution of any nation in times of stress and danger such as we now recall depends on its youth; depends ultimately perhaps on its *educated* youth. The voice of reason may be a gentle one, but it does not rest until it has gained a hearing. The things of the mind and of the spirit are inconspicuous in comparison with physical forces; they may be discounted by some in the logic of the day; but in the logic of the years it is the forces of mind and spirit which have prevailed. Let a nation seek honestly to live by righteousness and then it will go to war only for a righteous cause, one that is not

87

incompatible with the Christian conscience and the Christian faith.

The Christian conscience – ennobling a man so that he will give everything for others – "Greater love hath no man than this, that a man lay down his life for his friends".

And if the Christian conscience sometimes falters or is unsure, *the Christian faith:* "I am persuaded that neither death nor life . . . shall be able to separate us from the love of God, which is in Christ Jesus our Lord".

"ACCOUNTED WORTHY"

Strathallan School; 2nd October, 1949

"Accounted worthy to obtain that world . . . They cannot die any more"—Luke 20.35–36

The words come from the sermon which cost Jesus His life. It is the parable of the vineyard and the wicked husbandmen who killed, one after another, the servants of their master and finally his own son. Plainly and deliberately, Jesus told His enemies the truth about their own hearts, and from that moment His death at their hands was certain.

But it was probably something else that had brought the people into church that morning. The church was crowded. It had gone abroad that there was to be a discussion about the life to come. The Sadducees did not believe in any resurrection, and they were there in force to argue with Jesus: and a great congregation was there to listen. It was not, I imagine, from curiosity. That may have brought one or two; but most of them came out of a deep hunger. They wanted to know about the world beyond. It was all dark to them. People will listen to someone who has light to shed on this subject. The hardest man of the world may try to persuade himself that he is content with this earthly life; but there come to him at times misgivings that cannot be silenced, and they may even grow to a haunting fear. Here in Scotland we recall the refrain of William Dunbar's poem:

Timor mortis conturbat me

The fear of death doth trouble us.

On the other side, there are those who realise, as time

goes by, that they have many dear friends in that other world; and it is becoming real to them with the reality of intimate affection. Indeed, compared with the world that is to come, *this* world is a very tiny parish. "Take in the dead, and who are in the majority?" By comparison, our little earth dwindles away into a point of light. Seen from the walls of Heaven it must seem only a "fretful midge", nothing more. If we are wise, we do not send our roots very deep down here. We are like the man living in the Far East who knows that in a little while he will be going home. He rightly interests himself in the life around him and willingly spends himself for the community; yet he knows that his real home is not there but across the water, whence he first came.

We are all eager to hear anything new about that world which is our rightful home. Nowadays there are few of us, old or young, who have not a friend called away to that far land. We remember loved ones from our homes whose memory is imprinted on our hearts; or friends who died by our side, when we were strangely spared; or those who loved this school where they were nurtured, and brought honour to it by their courage.

Perhaps Jesus disappointed some of the congregation that day. He called no spirits back to chatter about their happiness. He did not even draw a picture of the other world. When people came to Him perplexed about these matters, Jesus always spoke to them quietly about God. We can understand why He did that. When a man comes home after long exile, he does not spend his time wondering about the state of his house or his garden. He is thinking of one who will be there to welcome him. Jesus knew that we should not be greatly helped by the description or the measurements of Heaven. "The Father's House" – that is description enough. "God Himself shall be with them and be their God." When asked about the world to come, Jesus spoke about God.

Secondly, in speaking of that other world, Jesus refers to its "Roll of Honour" – "those who are accounted worthy to obtain that world". Perhaps we should rather say "Roll of Service", for we feel that they are not resting on their laurels but remembering us and helping us. Things happen that feel like the touch of familiar hands. They are not far away.

"Accounted worthy" – how Jesus can take a word and transform it! He takes, for example, the word "love", which before was only the name for an incident in our fleeting human experience, and with Him it becomes the name for the pre-occupation of eternity. So here He takes the word "worth", which for us is a word of the market-place ("What is he worth?" some ask, meaning only "How much money does he have?") and makes of it a name for the eternal things, the things that cannot be bought with a price, and that do not die with death.

This afternoon we are each remembering our own; but we are linking their memory with courage and nobility in all lands and all ages. There are two features which mark out such courage and nobility. One is that which the historian records of Nelson; his *dedication*. On such a day as this – in October, 1805 – the Admiral came to Downing Street to say good-bye on his way to meet the French and Spanish fleets at Trafalgar. The shy, austere Prime Minister, who shared the same unselfish love for his country, showed his recognition of it by waiting on him to his carriage – an honour he would not have paid to a royal prince. The real core of the great seaman, he felt, was his absolute self-surrender. That will always win men's reverence. It has inspired those whom we remember today to do that "which the world may talk of hereafter"; that which perhaps wins no headlines, but might be the theme of a ballad.

The Roll of the Worthy – we use another phrase for it

sometimes, and it startles us to recall that we too are inscribed on it – The Communion of Saints. The Christian Church is the Communion of Saints on earth. We meet together Sunday by Sunday, a company of people who have heard that Christ is to pass this way. We gather here because this is one of the places that He has promised to visit. And it is good to recall that we are only "the rear ranks of a vast procession winding its way through the centuries; that we as yet are still in the shadow, look yonder, how they pass into the glory of the sunlight, row on row".

Nevertheless, simply to come here is not to be counted worthy. You do not come into the Kingdom by drifting. There is a test, a trial, a judgment, by which the worthy are separated out. We hear again the warning words, "Take heed that the vineyard be not given to others". No one ever drifted into Heaven. That way lies upstream not down. And at once we say in our hearts, "I am not to be accounted worthy". Rightly so, and inevitably; but we are glad that the last word on this matter is not with us. Many great souls in the past have spoken as we must speak. There was Jacob: "I am not worthy of the least of all Thy mercies". There was John the Baptist: "I am not worthy to stoop down and unloose His shoes". There was the Roman centurion: "I am not worthy that Thou shouldst come under my roof". There was the Prodigal: "I am not worthy to be called thy son". And today there is the Indian poet whose hymn we sing:

> So weak am I, O gracious Lord,
> So all unworthy Thee,
> That even the dust upon Thy feet
> Outweighs me utterly.

God undertakes to change all this if only we will have it

so. The way into the Kingdom is by effort not by drift; but there comes a time when men feel that they are not swimming but sinking; not making headway but losing distance. The current is overpowering. It is then that there happens the most wonderful thing of all. God comes, like a strong swimmer to a man in peril of his life, whose struggles are only sending him deeper down; and behold, as soon as we are willing to trust Him, we are safe. As we honour those who were accounted worthy to obtain that world, we ask, can we in our turn be worthy?

Yes! Not in our own strength, but in the strength which God offers.

> O Saviour, I have nought to plead,
> In earth beneath or heaven above,
> But just my own exceeding need
> And Thy exceeding love.

REMEMBRANCE BETWEEN TWO WARS

St. Anne's Church, Edinburgh; 12th November, 1933

"To what purpose is this waste?"—Matthew 26.8

The thoughts of many go back to the day on which the guns ceased fire and the world threw off the nightmare of the war. If you return today to the battlefields of France and Flanders, you will find that Nature has been quietly and surely covering the traces of it; strewing the battlefields with corn and grass and flowers; obliterating the memory of it. Nature has forgotten. We cannot forget.

> At the going down of the sun, and in the morning,
> We will remember them.

Sometimes, perhaps, we hear the old question: To what purpose is this waste? What good has the war done? some people ask. Of course we know that the waste should never have been. Into a Christian world the war could not have come. In the same way the death of Jesus should never have happened. Into a good world He would have come only to reign.

To what purpose is this waste? some people ask. The question, as St. John tells us, was asked not by the disciples in general, *but by Judas*. The story of this beautiful act by Mary is understood only if we look at its setting – the events that went before it and the events that followed. The first few verses of the chapter tell of the meeting of the chief priests and the scribes to plot the death of Jesus. The verses which follow the story tell of Judas going out – the complaint still on his lips that three hundred pence had been wasted on Jesus – going out to betray Him for one hundred pence.

96

Here, then, is the context. First, Mary's act arose out of the threat of the danger that was menacing Jesus. There was the Appeal and the Response. Second, the act itself was a Costly Sacrifice which counted not the cost. Third, its issue was the Betrayal. That is the solemn Warning.

These three movements are here in the story of sacrifice that we recall today.

1. There was *Appeal and Response*. All things that were dearest to men were in jeopardy – home and kindred and country, justice and righteousness. When we find that our enemies felt the same appeal, that does not detract from the heroism, though it deepens the tragedy. We should remember, at this Commemoration season, that in Germany too, men and women are holding the festival of the war-dead; that in commemoration services in central Europe the same cries go up to Heaven for son and brother, for father and friend, "O death where is thy sting, O grave where is thy victory?" And again in resignation, "Thy will be done". In the torn country of Alsace-Lorraine there were set up, after the war, memorials like our own, but with a difference. Each has two panels for the names of the fallen. On one there is a list of names headed by the inscription, "These men fell for their country, fighting in the army of France". The other has a list of names too, and the inscription, "These men fell for their country, fighting in the army of Germany". And every man felt that his country was in danger and called on him.

Many soldiers found it easy to face death. "If I die", they said, "I die doing what I know to be right and good, for at least once in my life. Death could not find me at a better time." More than that – they came to see that death was not the awe-inspiring and solemn event that it becomes when looked at through the mists of daily life. At home death enters very seldom into our lives: we forget that it is the

97

inevitable thing. There it happened hourly, and because men were not tied any longer closely to the things of the world, death had lost its sting. Men, going into battle, made light of their coming passion. You found them, even on leave – in the brief glorious respite – filled with a strange uncontrollable stirring at the heart to be back, sharing it with their friends. Once and for all they had deliberately surrendered this world and all it held most dear. They were living already in an unearthly world apart. You saw it even in the little, pathetic, tragic renunciations, that stopped short of the giving of life itself. There is an incident recorded by Henri Barbusse in his book, *Le Feu*. (It was one of the earliest war books. It appeared in 1916. And hardly one since has come near to it in verisimilitude.) A soldier in the author's platoon went home on leave. It was the glorious reunion to which he had looked forward for eighteen months. Before he went off to the Front, he had been married and in that year-and-a-half he had not seen his young wife again. Arriving home, he found a telegram waiting for him at the station. He was recalled. His battalion was going back into action. Instead of a fortnight, he had only a few precious hours. But in the railway station he encountered four soldiers, stranded for the night and unable to find shelter. It was a night of terrible wind and rain. They must come with him, he said, to the little café still run by his wife – all that was left of it by an air-raid. After some hot coffee, he would find shelter for them. It proved impossible to find any lodging. Even the café had only the one room left. And the cellars were knee-deep in water. Those few precious hours, which might never be repeated, that young couple gave to these stranded men. They never spoke of the sacrifice they were making. Sometimes they caught each other's eyes, and saw perfect understanding. *This* was the only right thing. That was the fellowship of these years. It was made possible because men felt, perhaps only in a dim and perplexed fashion, that the things of Christ were in jeopardy.

2. There was *Costly Sacrifice which did not count the cost*. Sometimes, perhaps, our proud thanksgiving changes for a moment to the old, sore questioning, the sense of the sheer folly of it; the waste of so much that was precious. Those whom we remember were so young. Their lives seemed hardly to have begun. Why were they withdrawn so prematurely? We know part of the answer when we remember that this world is only a place for the fashioning and testing of character: a vale of soul-making.

Since the war, many a life has centred round a far off grave. A few years after the war, I had the opportunity of revisiting the battlefields of the Ypres Salient. Houses stood where once there had been only shell-holes: and streets ran where once there were only trenches. Not a single feature of that former landscape could be identified again. But at one point I found a gravestone that had escaped all the storms of war. It had been there in the days of battle and was still unremoved. Round that fixed point it was easy to trace the outlines of those days. Round this grave everything fell into place. In how many hearts today is that the case? All the world falls into place round a grave. It may be that it is only an empty grave, a cenotaph, because your hallowed ground cannot be identified. Remember then that Christianity itself was built on an empty grave: on the cenotaph of Jesus; on that grave which stood trimphantly empty on the first Easter Day.

3. Mary's gracious act issued in the departure of Judas to betray Christ. There follows *the Warning*. As the sight of that chivalrous deed was darkness and not light to Judas, and drove him out to hasten his deed of shame, so there were those who re-acted to the chivalry of war-time only by learning to make

99

profit out of man's necessity. So today there are those who become a warning – all those who cannot or will not make peace on earth; all those who, for one reason or another, for hatred or greed or national pride, still cling to the ancient state of things, and invent plausible excuses.

Wherever, said Jesus, the Gospel shall be preached in the whole world, the deed of this woman shall be a memorial of her. Wherever the sacrificial deeds of fathers and brothers and sons and daughters are spoken of, in the whole world, there let their memorial be peace on earth, and the brotherhood which they made in the valley of the shadow.

AN ACKNOWLEDGEMENT: A BOOK:
A SACRAMENT

COLLEGIATE CHURCH OF ST. SALVATOR;
11TH NOVEMBER, 1956

"By way of remembrance"—II Peter 3.1

For the seniors of our University this day of remembrance recalls, most of all, the critical period of 1940 when in the Springtime so many of our graduates and our students were giving their lives; when many known to us were being surrounded in the Fifty-First (Highland) Division at St. Valery and carried into a long captivity.

At home the Chiefs of Staff were preparing their report for the Cabinet. Here is the last paragraph of their appreciation: "Our conclusion is that *prima facie* Germany has most of the cards; but the real test is whether the morale of our fighting personnel and civil population will counter-balance the numerical and material advantages which Germany enjoys. We believe it will."

Those of us, however, who have kept this day for ten years now, since the end of the war, must realise (it is an effort to do it) that, for the bejant year, Dunkirk, for instance, is not even a memory, but European history. True, it is likely to be, for them also, both tragic and gallant history, since they can almost certainly count among their family some who took part in it, some perhaps who gave their lives then. It is right to remember, on this day set apart, those who fought and died in two World Wars, and those who since then have given their lives in opposing terrorism and tyranny.

It *is* Remembrance Day. Other themes too we must keep in mind – United Nations, Disarmament, Peace, those who are suffering at this very hour under cruel oppression – but today is the day for remembering those who gave their lives for us. The act of silence is our solemn acknowledgement. How did it take that form? Perhaps from the lifting of the barrage on the enemy's trench-system (I can go back in memory to that typical experience of 1914–1918) when perhaps in the sudden, incredible hush, you might hear a sky-lark singing in the blue heaven above, or you might have vivid memories of home, and so for a fleeting moment or two be able to recall that there was a world made by God and seen to be good; that there is still the peace and the love nurtured in the hearts of good people everywhere. Or we may now associate the silence with the end of a bombing-attack, when the danger is past, but the losses are still to be reckoned.

This silent remembrance is, first, *an acknowledgement*. "The righteous shall be in everlasting remembrance." (Psalm 112.6.) They would be surprised to hear themselves called by that lofty word, but if it means "right with God, merciful and self-forgetful", then we have justification in claiming the text for them. In courage and loyalty and sacrifice there is something that cannot be refuted or gainsaid, as you learned from the peasants of Normandy when the landings of 1944 took place. Our assaults disrupted their lives (long attuned to the presence and the pattern of an occupying army); they destroyed their homes and threatened their bodies; yet you found them tending the lonely graves of those who had fallen in the first waves across the beaches; adopting them and placing fresh flowers every morning.

Remembrance extends not to those alone who died in battle, but to the countless millions who perished in concentration camps like Buchenwald or Ravensbrück; and the desolate ones who died as homeless refugees. There is no end to the roll-call. In Paris alone by the Spring of 1944 the number of people taken by the Gestapo was greater than the total number of deaths in the air raids on London; and a large percentage of those taken by the Gestapo were tortured. For a year the head of the Resistance (Monsieur Bidault), an office which he had courageously undertaken after his predecessor had been captured and executed, had to live underground, sleeping in a different place every night. Men and women were aware of the tragic dilemma : the only way to make peace was to resort to arms.

Our remembrance, secondly, takes the form of *a Book*. It rests here in its shrine behind this pulpit in which John Knox once preached. It holds the names of all the members of the University who gave their lives in the Second World War, and the inscription round it continues the tribute above our mosaic memorial of the First World War – *Mox et eorum:* "And now in memory of those who in another war poured out their lives, whose names are here written in a Book". It was on a morning of September, 1950, on the five hundredth anniversary of the founding of St. Salvator's College by Bishop Kennedy, that Queen Elizabeth, now the Queen Mother, unveiled the shrine "To the glory of God and in memory of the members of this University who laid down their lives". As the Union Jack fell from the shrine, the draping of the memorial windows behind was removed and the interior of this lovely building was flooded with light and colour. Every Sunday morning during term-time the student-reader of the Scripture lesson enters before the congregation has assembled and turns a fresh page of the Book of Remembrance. Thus the Roll is called without ceasing. We keep an everlasting remembrance. In an introduction to the Roll of Honour, Principal Sir James Irvine wrote (and we remember that the name of his only son stands on the Roll), "St. Andrews is more than a University : she is in truth *Alma Mater* to those whom she has nourished, and it is as Rachel sorrowing for her children that she mourns the untimely loss of these young lives cut short in the first fine flower of youth. Thus it comes that our Roll of Honour is no mere register of names; it carries the abiding love and proud grief of a stricken mother. No member of the University can ever forget the courageous spirit in which our young men and women followed where duty called them. Casting aside all thought of self or of future, with a full realisation of the toil, endurance and danger which lay before them, they turned from the work for which they had prepared themselves by years of study to the task of combating tyranny by force of arms. They went with the knowledge that they might never return – that the one would be taken and the other left – and now they are with us still but only as a bright example shining in loving memory. This record will be cherished in many a home and a special copy will be preserved in the University Chapel where our children worshipped in the golden days of student-dom and where their successors will gain touch with the values which are eternal. Each day a page of this book will be turned so that the Roll of Honour will be called without ceasing. Their strife is over and we who are left must not fail them. May we in turn earn in part, as they have earned so fully, the right to have applied to us the proudest of all tributes – 'Well done, good and faithful servant, enter thou into the joy of thy Lord'."

Thus our special remembrance in the University centres on a Book of Remembrance.

Finally, our remembrance recalls *a sacrament*. "This do", Jesus said in the Upper Room, the night before He died, "in remembrance of me". It was said by St. Paul that "The Jews require a sign, and the Greeks seek after wisdom : but we preach Christ crucified" (1 Cor. 1.22f.). As it has been translated, "The Jews want a miracle, and the Greeks want an argument". But Jesus refused these. Instead He gave Himself to be crucified, without using His heavenly powers to evade death. In the end, neither miracle nor argument is finally convincing; but sacrifice *is*. And we cannot help remembering today that all true sacrifice, loyalty and courage are of God.

It was surprising to find a recent Gifford lecturer falling into a familiar trap. Quoting a Father Fitzgerald in comment on his general, "He was a great soldier, a great Christian, and a great gambler", he caps it with the childish phrase, "*Life is a gamble*". We ought to realise that if a man is a great gambler he cannot at the same time be either a great soldier or a great Christian. There are many aspects of warfare in which the military art has now become an exact science and no general officer worthy of the name would commit his troops to battle at a peradventure, in the hope that some run of luck will see him through and save his reputation; and the Christian faith does not deal in chance and in perhapses: it proclaims the great redeeming act of God in the sacrifice of His Son for us sinful men; and so announces divine and certain assurance. This morning again Christ speaks to us across the centuries, saying, "This I have done, remembering you: this do in remembrance of me". Nor is it only on Remembrance Day, or on Communion Sunday, that we are to remember. Not even on Sunday only. "Seven whole days", says George Herbert:

> Seven whole days, not one in seven,
> I will praise Thee.

Every day! – the happy days and the sad days too. One writer said recently that most people live either by memory or by hope; that the present is rarely exciting or stimulating. I think, with most of you, that just the opposite is true. Even when there is no crisis in world-affairs the present is vivid and absorbing and crammed with interest. Nevertheless, it is because of memory and it is because of hope that you can live securely in the present. Take memory away and much is lost. Take hope away and all is lost: the bright day is done and we are for the dark. We live in the present in the solemn remembrance of God's redeeming act and in His assurance of eternal life offered to us in Him.

> Praise the Lord! For He is glorious;
> Never shall His promise fail;
> God hath made His saints victorious;
> Sin and death shall not prevail.

"THE GLORY AND THE SCANDAL
OF THE UNIVERSE"

University of St. Andrews; 9th November, 1941

"And Moses took the bones of Joseph with him : for he had straitly sworn the children of Israel, saying, 'God will surely visit you ; and ye shall carry up my bones away hence with you.'"
—Exodus 13.19

An expeditionary force setting out today moves rapidly by rail and road and air, in trains, lorries, tanks, troop-carriers, transport-planes ; but when infantry divisions made that trek from Egypt into Palestine half a century ago, their difficulties were not very different from those of the Israelites. First under General Murray and then under Lord Allenby, the Egyptian Expeditionary Force was faced by severe problems of logistics. The recurrent command was, "Lighten the load : be mobile". When orders came for a sudden move, to march or to fight, all the baggage that was not absolutely essential had to be left behind. The children of Israel marched in haste. They moved by night. To many in that company of people as yet un-disciplined by the rigours of desert life, this casket with the remains of their ancestors must have seemed a queer piece of lumber to carry on a long journey. Their leader, they may have felt, would have employed his time better in pre-paring transport and stores for the march. Of what use to them on their hazardous journey was this memorial of a dead man ? There would be a good deal of grumbling in the ranks.

Moses took the bones of Joseph with him. It was the dying man's own wish. He had an honourable grave in Egypt, a Prince's tomb ; but there was a thing for which he longed far more – when the time came (and he foresaw the change in the fortunes of his people) his bones should be carried up with them on their march into the unknown.

Today *we* are joining in an act of piety and faith, commemorating those who, in two wars, have died for us. Perhaps we have stood by their graves, those shallow graves hastily dug by weary men in the lull of a battle and marked by a rough-hewn cross of wood; or in the vast cemeteries of Flanders and the Somme, where the little monuments stand in row upon row; or by the cenotaph on the Menin Gate in honour of those whose graves are unknown (yet their name liveth for evermore); or by the war-memorial, of city and village, or here by the sacred panels honouring those, *olim cives,* who have gone ahead of us. Once a year we record our determination to do something more; to carry with us into the future the memory and the inspiration of the dead. Joseph was always a dreamer, but his last dream was the best, a vision of the future of his people. Those whom we remember today once dreamed of the things which they might achieve with their lives; but perhaps *their* last dream was the best also. When they saw that the future was not for them, they dreamed of the great things that *we* should do when they were gone.

That casket was a mark of faith. "By faith", we read, "Joseph when he died gave commandment concerning his bones." Our dead had faith in God and in the better future He would bring into being out of calamity; and they had also – a braver and bolder faith – faith in us and all that *we* might do.

For their sakes, then, there are three things that we shall consider.

1. *The Shame of War.* Once again it has been shown for what it is, as rational and as admirable as a riot with broken bottles. If there were still any who dreamed idly of the romance of war, as did Rupert Brooke and Compton Mackenzie on the way to Gallipoli, they were soon dis-

illusioned. The grim reality is made up mostly of unutterable weariness, of bitter cold and bitter wounds, of sand-storm and desert heat, of death in terrible forms, of destruction by mine and bomb and torpedo. Most tragic of all is the shame of the young lives that are lost; the brave thoughts; the ideals; the affections that have perished from the earth. It is always youth that suffers most, for it is youth that presses on most impetuously and unselfishly. Man, said Pascal, is the glory and the scandal of the universe. This thing, that man can bring upon the world, is the nadir of the scandal.

2. *"The glory and the scandal."* Is there any *glory* left? Strangely, from a business that seems sheer evil, God in His grace can bring forth good. We are right in laying on the war-memorial a wreath of laurel, *a crown of glory.* There is the glory of *righteousness,* the satisfaction that, if we must enter into this, we do it with clean hands. That conviction gives nobility to the most ordinary of men. I think of a Scottish battalion which was the spearhead of the British advance into Belgium on 10th May, 1940. (We are proud to welcome back one of our own students who was a leader of these men, and is now recovering from his severe wounds.) They were men who got into endless trouble and mischief in the days of waiting; but when the test came they covered themselves with glory that will never be recorded. After a few days fighting their flanks were in the air – and that is no mere technical term: it may mark the difference between living and dying. Then came the final message by radio from battalion headquarters: "We are surrounded, but giving as good as we get". Then, soon afterwards, silence. The story of Dunkirk shows once again that these men, who have little regard for the exploits that make newspaper headlines, have, in their own humble way, an unspoiled instinct for those things which would go well in a ballad. So the second glory

is the glory of *consecrated heroism*. It was often heroism unseen and unknown. Naturally, the bravest ventures have no chronicler; those who go out may never come back to tell of them; but God does not look His soldiers over for medals, but for scars. There are epics which no man can write – of fateful watches in the Atlantic; of the little ships of Dunkirk and that imperishable rearguard action; of the women who have lost their homes, with all they had in the world – except their courage; of those who, when our bombers go out, lie awake till the darkness thins again, to listen, and to count the number that return. Here, in our University, we have a part of chastened pride in those annals. We hear of one of our graduates, a doctor, staying on day after day on the beaches, while the hopes of rescue quickly fade, and attending to the wounded to the end. He is still "missing". And of another, also "missing", of whom a prisoner has written, "He was last seen leading his platoon in a charge : the men would have followed him anywhere". Our age will be retrieved by the heroism of such as these, and by the silent courage of those who wait at home. It is a hard discipline; but it is surer than indifference. Rust will crumble a metal when hammer blows will only harden it.

3. The laurels on our wreath are the symbol of glory : the poppies stand for *sacrifice* – the poppies which will always recall the fields of Flanders. They speak of something even beyond heroism. Before the onslaught came in May, 1940, it was noticed by everyone in France that it was the most beautiful springtime that anyone could remember, bright with primroses and cowslips, with golden gorse and delicate apple-blossom. Could any punishment be too harsh for the evil men whose lust was to desecrate and shatter that ethereal loveliness? Perhaps to the man without strong faith it was merely pathetic – as if God were above and around, but quite power-

113

less to intervene? Something more was needed; something beyond physical and mental exaltation which of themselves might inspire courage. That something is recalled today, that self-sacrifice which speaks of the presence of God *in human souls*. In time of war we have a new understanding of the Cross of Christ. The story is told of a medical officer. He was not a deeply religious man; but once, after a battle, a number of severely wounded cases were brought into his C.C.S. He was a veteran soldier and had seen suffering in many forms, but by the pathos of these cases he was deeply moved. "This sort of thing", he said, "makes me want to suffer everything for everyone once and get it over." In a few words he expressed the Christian instinct. "Greater love hath no man than this, that a man lay down his life for his friends."

> O deathless dead, who do not die,
> Save as Christ died upon the Cross!

Our own young comrades have shared in the Christian sacrifice. We grow old: they abide. "Age shall not weary them, nor the years condemn."

"Now just as the Gates were opened to let in the men, I looked in after them; and behold the City shone like the Sun. . . . And after that they shut up the Gates: which, when I had seen, I wished myself among them."

PRAYER
Grant us grace fearlessly to contend against evil, and to make no peace with aggression; and, that we may reverently use our freedom, help us to employ it in the maintenance of justice among men and nations.

"ONE OF THE FEW"

UNIVERSITY OF ST. ANDREWS; 11TH NOVEMBER, 1951

In an age such as ours, in which we emphasise the present world to the almost complete exclusion of the other, it is of the first importance to keep fresh our remembrance of whence we come and whither we go. This is a season set apart for remembrance – of those who have gone this way before us, and have passed into the world of light; and especially this is the day on which we remember those known to ourselves, called from this world, as it seemed prematurely, whom we remember Sunday by Sunday in the simple ceremony of turning a fresh page in our Book of Remembrance.

It has frequently been said that no one knows what the leisured, happy life of man can be who cannot recall the halcyon days of the world as it was before 1914. I should like to lay alongside that saying what I take to be a more important comment: No one will ever know the real nature of human friendship, of courage and of sacrifice who did not experience these in the setting of the World Wars or similar circumstances challenging the human spirit. It is right that we should recall these things very often with thanksgiving; for when we bow our heads in sorrow with those who mourn their lost loved ones, we must record and cherish those proud achievements for which they gave all that they had to give.

With today's Remembrance Service in mind, I was thinking of all this on a still autumn evening in Northern France. The rich harvest fields slipped past the window of the railway-carriage, white and clear under a full moon. These scenes were familiar to two generations of our students, who fought and died in such surroundings, separated by three decades. The intervening years seemed to fall away. The nightly patrols of the long routine of trench-warfare took their place beside the raid on Dieppe and the storming of the Normandy beaches. Here was a common battleground. Here were features familiar to the patient infantry of 1914 and to the impetuous commando of thirty years later. As I watched that historic landscape flow past, there were held vividly in my mind three incidents of the previous three days, personal experiences, deeply moving in themselves, and yet more than personal because they were symbolic of the thoughts and emotions which we all shared in those fateful days and share once again this morning as we reverently recall the past.

First was a visit to one who as a young tank officer in the French Army escaped from enemy hands by swimming the River Loire; who became a leader in the Resistance movement, was betrayed, and endured two years of Buchenwald. Amid the horror and brutality of it, the greatest strain on his Christian faith was the complete, utter absence of kindliness. In those who had control over their lives, there was no vestige of pity. To such depths human depravity can descend. Here, in vivid and terrifying reality, are set before our eyes the causes, the nature, and the consequences of war. The causes – greed, love of dominance, lust for power. The nature of it – the innocent suffer, cruelty is unleashed, ideals perish. The consequences of it – fear, misery, despair, death. Where men died in tens and hundreds of thousands, my friend survived, one of the few who came out comparatively unscathed in mind and spirit.

The second incident was a visit to the little town of Veule-les-Roses, a quiet holiday resort on the coast of Normandy, living its own placid life till war rushed down on it; then, in one memorable night, suddenly linked imperishably with the fortunes of Scottish soldiers caught in the tide of battle. A large part of the 51st (Highland) Division was fighting a rearguard action, with ammunition running out and the escape-route rapidly narrowing: to a few resolute men came the happy chance of saving something from the disaster. The small harbour was already occupied, but the great chalk cliffs, 300 feet high, were still unguarded. While cautious signals were exchanged with naval vessels waiting out at sea, the perilous descent was made. We see what can be achieved by human courage, training, initiative, persistence, and the refusal to give in. The operation was successful. By looping rifle-slings together, a rope was made long enough to secure a safe outcome. But it could be only a limited success; only the escape from immediate danger. It was a most brilliant achievement; but it was negative. These men came safely out, but to gain their final purpose, they knew that men must one day return. Courage, training, initiative, persistence, the refusal to give in – all are needed still, and greatly needed; but now there must be combined with these the disciplined readiness to offer everything again if need be. One day these men, and many others like them, must return to Europe, in that calm resolution that sends men into battle without regrets, without any looking back over the shoulder. John Masefield described it in unforgettable phrases for that battle of the First World War in which many of our students fell, a battle which took seventy thousand lives in its opening day.

"The hand of Time rested on the half-hour mark, and along all that old front line . . . there came a whistling and a crying. The men of the first wave climbed up the parapets, in tumult, darkness, and the presence of death, and having done with all pleasant things, advanced across No Man's Land to begin the Battle of the Somme."

And a Scottish soldier and leader of men wrote memorable words about the North African campaign of the Second War, thinking of that hour of dawn when the man on active service

watches the mists rise over the enemy's lines, and when his
thoughts turn as always homewards, and, it may well be, for
the last time. In those far off homes, they are being remembered at that hour.

> To those dear houses with their chimneys reeking
> In Angus or in Fife,
> No spirit came, its words of omen speaking,
> To mother or to wife;
> Yet in the homeless desert to the southward
> Before the sun was high,
> The husbands whom they love, the sons they mothered
> Stood up and went to die.
>
> (BERNARD FERGUSSON : *Towards the East*)

The scene of return, in that spirit of self-forgetting, in June
of 1944, was the third experience still vividly in my mind. At
Courseulles, and along Juno and Gold beaches, all was swept
clean as it had been seven years ago – then, because every
scrap of metal was precious and could be used for something;
now, because the beaches have returned to their former purpose of serving the holiday-maker, and every irrelevant thing
has gone. There was, however, one scrap of memory – a clip
that once had held five rounds of small arms ammunition. It was
easy to visualise its brief history – the fight for fire superiority
on the beach; the quick recharging of the magazine before
the attack goes in on the fortified sand-dune; the charger
ground into the sand as the man rises to go forward. Did he
survive? Or did he give his life that day in the dunes for the
liberation of Europe? At least I know that because men were
ready to give up everything in that hour, my friend far off in
Buchenwald was to be set free. There is no one-to-one
equation; but the broad principle is there – without shedding

of blood there is no victory, no liberation, no peace.

The link with the Christian faith is very plain. Because man has endured the perils of war and has learned its strange and inescapable lessons, he can better understand what God is saying to the world in the coming of Jesus. The *thought* of God becoming man; the *idea* of a world-saviour – these are thrilling and haunting and exciting speculations; but, if they remain as thoughts, as ideas, they will not save any souls. Mithraism had the legend of a world-saviour, but nothing more; and it was because Christianity had *the fact* of the Saviour to offer needy men that Christianity had nothing to fear from so powerful an adversary.

At the critical stage of a famous battle, the son of the army commander, who was serving as a subaltern under his father, saw how a quick tactical success could be attained and approached the general to suggest the plan by which the enemy's strong-point could be seized and held with the sacrifice of a very few men. The general – it was Quintus Fabius Maximus – at once asked, "Are you ready to be one of the few?"

Jesus was prepared to be the One. So every Sunday is a Day of Remembrance of His redemptive love and of His victory over sin and death when He rose again on this first day of the week. His life and death and resurrection have given new significance to all human loyalty and striving. The courage and training and initiative of man, his persistence in the face of danger and his refusal to give in – all of these, even when readiness to sacrifice everything has been added, may yet be deceptive. Dictators have been able to evoke them all for sinister purposes. It is the spirit in which these are used that matters in the end, and the cause to which they are dedicated. Are they consecrated to the service of God and none other – neither self, nor nation, but God who judges self and nation? All these, by themselves, are precarious: offered to God, they are the glory of mankind.

O Father of all, we remember before Thee those whom we love but see no longer. To Thine eternal faithfulness and love we commend them and all who are dear to us, through Jesus Christ Thy Son. Amen.

"RISE UP YE DEAD"

St. Cuthbert's Church, Lockerbie;
6th November, 1932

"These all died in faith, not having received the promises, but having seen them afar off . . . and confessed that they were strangers and pilgrims on the earth. For they . . . declare plainly that they seek a country . . . Now they desire a better country, that is, an heavenly"—Hebrews 11.13–16

When the French Army was hard pressed by the enemy, a soldier called Jacques Pericard cried to the prostrate forms in the trench, *"Debout les Morts!"* It was a fine cry, and it was echoed throughout all France. It was a cry of loneliness, "Rise up ye dead !" *Their* help was taken away when it was most needed.

"Rise up ye dead !" It is in this time of strain that we miss them most. They were the bravest, the most gifted; they should have been the leaders today. If they were to come back this morning, while we think of them, would they feel that we have finished the work which they began? Or would they say, "The struggle nought availeth; The labour and the wounds are vain"? Not, I am sure, if we can show that we have proved loyal.

1. First, we have their memory, and we pray that we may not prove disloyal to it. It is well to keep them in mind. There is enough of tragedy in the world that cannot be excluded from our thoughts; enough carelessness and indifference; enough vice and sin. It is good to turn back to one thing that is likely to make our era *immortal* – the heroism of those who died then.

"A strange period", the historian may say of this half-century, "a period of lavish spending and gay living, side by side with serious poverty and bitter distress; but look closer.

They lived carelessly, but see how they could die." Already the historian is suggesting this. Our age will rightly be blamed for many follies, but the courage with which those days were faced may retrieve us. R. H. Gretton has written about the riches of bravery and sacrifice packed into one little scene that could be witnessed almost any night during four years of war, 1914–1918. The leave-trains at Victoria Station, he says, have never found their poet. The soldiers returning to the Front had to leave their friends at the barrier. "With pack and equipment, bayonets and entrenching tools, mess-tins and haversacks, and rifles slung on a shoulder, clumsy in their heavy greatcoats, medieval in the sleeveless leather jerkins and the flattish steel helmets . . . they looked entirely creatures of some other life . . . It was as if that half-secret, underground world of the front line, which grew, in place of grass and hedges, sordid stumps and rusty wire and rotting rags of men, had produced a new race of the right shape to live in it – ponderous little dinosaurs of the battle slime. How much easier if they could have been thought so! But they were men." And, for the silent little groups left by the gateway, the platform had suddenly grown dreary and cruel. "The leave-trains of Victoria never found their poet."

Yes; our age may be retrieved by the sacrifice of many yonder, and by the silent courage of many at home.

There was more than heroism. Without trying to make saints of all who took part, we recognise that there was in all some dim faith that it was all part of the sufferings which might rescue the world. In the most critical hour in 1918 when Haig sent out his famous "Backs to the wall" message, he made no appeal to the baser passions of cruelty, hatred, or vengeance.

"There is no other course open to us but to fight it out. Every position must be held to the last man. There must be no retirement. With our backs to the wall and believing in the justice of our cause, each one of us must fight on to the end."

The message was published in orders on the morning of 12th April. It met with an instant response and an echo all along the line; for, however dimly, every man knew that life in this world was not all that mattered. One of the greatest of our war books puts it this way, "Maynard spied, lonely in a corner of a field, a gathering of wooden crosses. All young men, all young men! There must be something more important than life, thought Maynard, or else why are those boys there?"

2. "These all died in faith", says this verse from the letter to the Hebrews, and the passage continues, "They desire a country, an heavenly country". Katherine Tynan once pictured the surprising transformation that had taken place in Heaven. As a rule it is the old and tired who arrive there: now it is suddenly stormed by crowds of laughing, cheerful youngsters, troops of them in every street. *We* grow old: *they* do not. When Rendel Harris was conducting a funeral service once, he looked round on the cemetery and exclaimed, "This is the emptiest place in all this city!" There are no dead. Another war book sets the truth in a simile which might appear trivial to others but which, the author says, every Englishman will understand. The beloved one who is gone is like a cricketer who has left the wickets, and though he has not yet laid aside bat and pads, "has finished with the game and has only the sweet evening sunlight and leisure of restful watchfulness remaining". We know the influence of the watchful spectator, of one who is out of it but still watching and encouraging. Because their personal part is played, they are even more intensely interested. We are compassed about with a cloud of witnesses.

3. *Behind us* are the things of memory. *Around us* are· the witnesses unseen. But we look also ahead. *Before us* are the promises. There must be more than sentiment. There must be active faith. They received not the promises, though they died to secure them. To them the dearest promise was *Peace*. If that does not come, the labour and the wounds are vain. It is the promise of the opening scenes of the Gospel. "Of all things", says Dante, "that are ordered to secure blessings to men, peace is the best. Hence the word which sounded to the shepherds from above was not riches, nor honour, nor length of life, nor health, nor strength, nor beauty; but peace . . . Therefore also, 'Peace be with you' was the salutation of the Saviour of mankind."

Dr. G. F. Barbour once summed it up by saying that our world was watching "a race between education and chaos"; but the Master and Guide of human life, who raised man so far above the lower creation and so wonderfully endowed him, will not lead us to the brink of catastrophe "without providing a means of crossing the gulf that yawns at our feet". If we are faithful, He will not permit those sacrifices to go for nothing. As there is one Saviour of the soul, there is one Saviour of the world. The hope, the only hope, the sure hope, lies in Christ the Lord.

Let us then keep fresh the memory of sacrifices made for us. Our lives, thus delivered, must be dedicated to a high purpose. We are called to the communion of the saints. A cloud of witnesses is around us. The spiritual world is very near, more real than the world we see. We desire a better country, that is a heavenly. They have attained. They wait for us.

All these were honoured in their generations
    and were the glory of their times.
There be of them that have left a name behind them
    that their praises might be reported :
And some there be which have no memorial ;
    who are perished as though they had never been,
And are become as though they had never been born :
    and their children after them.
But these were merciful men :
    whose righteousness hath not been forgotten.

Their bodies are buried in peace :
    but their name liveth for evermore.
The people shall tell of their wisdom :
    and the congregation will show forth their praise.

Ecclesiasticus 44.7–15